BARBARA KINGSOLVER

Critical Companions to Popular Contemporary Writers
Kathleen Gregory Klein, Series Editor

V. C. Andrews
by E. D. Huntley

Maya Angelou
by Mary Jane Lupton

Tom Clancy
by Helen S. Garson

Mary Higgins Clark
by Linda C. Pelzer

Arthur C. Clarke
by Robin Anne Reid

James Clavell
by Gina Macdonald

Pat Conroy
by Landon C. Burns

Robin Cook
by Lorena Laura Stookey

Michael Crichton
by Elizabeth A. Trembley

Howard Fast
by Andrew Macdonald

Ken Follett
by Richard C. Turner

Ernest J. Gaines
by Karen Carmean

John Grisham
by Mary Beth Pringle

James Herriot
by Michael J. Rossi

Tony Hillerman
by John M. Reilly

John Irving
by Josie P. Campbell

John Jakes
by Mary Ellen Jones

Jamaica Kincaid
by Lizabeth Paravisini-Gebert

Stephen King
by Sharon A. Russell

Dean Koontz
by Joan G. Kotker

Robert Ludlum
by Gina Macdonald

Anne McCaffrey
by Robin Roberts

Colleen McCullough
by Mary Jean DeMarr

James A. Michener
by Marilyn S. Severson

Toni Morrison
by Missy Dehn Kubitschek

Anne Rice
by Jennifer Smith

Tom Robbins
by Catherine E. Hoyser and Lorena Laura Stookey

John Saul
by Paul Bail

Erich Segal
by Linda C. Pelzer

Amy Tan
by E. D. Huntley

Anne Tyler
by Paul Bail

Leon Uris
by Kathleen Shine Cain

Gore Vidal
by Susan Baker and Curtis S. Gibson

BARBARA KINGSOLVER

A Critical Companion

Mary Jean DeMarr

CRITICAL COMPANIONS TO POPULAR CONTEMPORARY WRITERS
Kathleen Gregory Klein, Series Editor

Greenwood Press
Westport, Connecticut • London

Library of Congress Cataloging-in-Publication Data

DeMarr, Mary Jean, 1932–
   Barbara Kingsolver : a critical companion / Mary Jean DeMarr.
     p. cm.—(Critical companions to popular contemporary
writers, ISSN 1082–4979)
   Includes bibliographical references and index.
   ISBN 0-313-30638-9 (alk. paper)
   1. Kingsolver, Barbara—Criticism and interpretation. 2. Feminism
and literature—United States—History—20th century. 3. Women and
literature—United States—History—20th century. 4. Political
fiction, American—History and criticism. I. Title. II. Series.
PS3561.I496Z64 1999
813'.54—dc21   98–55347

British Library Cataloguing in Publication Data is available.

Library of Congress Catalog Card Number: 98–55347
ISBN: 0-313-30638-9
ISSN: 1082-4979

First published in 1999

Greenwood Press, 88 Post Road West, Westport, CT 06881
An imprint of Greenwood Publishing Group, Inc.
www.greenwood.com

Printed in the United States of America

The paper used in this book complies with the
Permanent Paper Standard issued by the National
Information Standards Organization (Z39.48–1984).

P

In order to keep this title in print and available to the academic community, this edition
was produced using digital reprint technology in a relatively short print run. This would
not have been attainable using traditional methods. Although the cover has been changed
from its original appearance, the text remains the same and all materials and methods used
still conform to the highest book-making standards.

*For the Bazaar Ladies—you know who you are!—
with thanks for friendship and support.*

Contents

Series Foreword

The authors who appear in the series Critical Companions to Popular Contemporary Writers are all best-selling writers. They do not simply have one successful novel, but a string of them. Fans, critics, and specialist readers eagerly anticipate their next book. For some, high cash advances and breakthrough sales figures are automatic; movie deals often follow. Some writers become household names, recognized by almost everyone.

But, their novels are read one by one. Each reader chooses to start and, more importantly, to finish a book because of what she or he finds there. The real test of a novel is in the satisfaction its readers experience. This series acknowledges the extraordinary involvement of readers and writers in creating a best-seller.

The authors included in this series were chosen by an Advisory Board composed of high school English teachers and high school and public librarians. They ranked a list of best-selling writers according to their popularity among different groups of readers. For the first series, writers in the top-ranked group who had received no book-length, academic, literary analysis (or none in at least the past ten years) were chosen. Because of this selection method, Critical Companions to Popular Contemporary Writers meets a need that is being addressed nowhere else. The success of these volumes as reported by reviewers, librarians, and teachers led to an expansion of the series mandate to include some writers with wide critical attention—Toni Morrison, John Irving, and Maya Angelou, for example—to extend the usefulness of the series.

The volumes in the series are written by scholars with particular expertise in analyzing popular fiction. These specialists add an academic focus to the popular success that these writers already enjoy.

The series is designed to appeal to a wide range of readers. The general reading public will find explanations for the appeal of these well-known writers. Fans will find biographical and fictional questions answered. Students will find literary analysis, discussions of fictional genres, carefully organized introductions to new ways of reading the novels, and bibliographies for additional research. Whether browsing through the book for pleasure or using it for an assignment, readers will find that the most recent novels of the authors are included.

Each volume begins with a biographical chapter drawing on published information, autobiographies or memoirs, prior interviews, and, in some cases, interviews given especially for this series. A chapter on literary history and genres describes how the author's work fits into a larger literary context. The following chapters analyze the writer's most important, most popular, and most recent novels in detail. Each chapter focuses on one or more novels. This approach, suggested by the Advisory Board as the most useful to student research, allows for an in-depth analysis of the writer's fiction. Close and careful readings with numerous examples show readers exactly how the novels work. These chapters are organized around three central elements: plot development (how the story line moves forward), character development (what the reader knows of the important figures), and theme (the significant ideas of the novel). Chapters may also include sections on generic conventions (how the novel is similar or different from others in its same category of science, fantasy, thriller, etc.), narrative point of view (who tells the story and how), symbols and literary language, and historical or social context. Each chapter ends with an "alternative reading" of the novel. The volume concludes with a primary and secondary bibliography, including reviews.

The alternative readings are a unique feature of this series. By demonstrating a particular way of reading each novel, they provide a clear example of how a specific perspective can reveal important aspects of the book. In the alternative reading sections, one contemporary literary theory—way of reading, such as feminist criticism, Marxism, new historicism, deconstruction, or Jungian psychological critique—is defined in brief, easily comprehensible language. That definition is then applied to the novel to highlight specific features that might go unnoticed or be understood differently in a more general reading. Each volume defines two or three specific theories, making them part of the reader's understanding of how diverse meanings may be constructed from a single novel.

Taken collectively, the volumes in the Critical Companions to Popular Contemporary Writers series provide a wide-ranging investigation of the complexities of current best-selling fiction. By treating these novels seriously as both literary works and publishing successes, the series demonstrates the potential of popular literature in contemporary culture.

Kathleen Gregory Klein
Southern Connecticut State University

Acknowledgments

Thanks, of course, to Kathy Klein for involving me in this project and to Barbara Rader for patiently bearing with questions and problems. Thanks also to Kathy Brooks and Donald Marshall for accurate and timely help with library research (and for falling in love with Kingsolver!), to Esther Russell for her eagle eye for reviews, and Sharon Russell for letting me talk through problems and issues.

1

Barbara Kingsolver:
Life and Works

Soft-spoken, in a quiet voice which shows clear traces of her Kentucky origins, Barbara Kingsolver impresses those who meet her with her gentleness and good humor. Paradoxically, however, she is a person of strong convictions which she is unafraid to voice and to live by, convictions which suffuse both her writings and her private life. A public person who values and strives to keep private her personal life, she avoids writing biographical fiction and yet she gives events and observations from her life to her characters, some of whom speak with voices rather similar to her own. A writer with a gift for telling engrossing stories and for creating interesting and lively characters, Kingsolver almost always begins working on each new piece of fiction with neither action nor character but rather with theme, with a question she wishes to examine. Unlike most serious writers, she considers herself a political writer, accepting that term, often considered a negative evaluation, with pleasure.

The basic facts about her life are quickly summarized. She was born in Annapolis, Maryland, on April 8, 1955, to Dr. Wendell R. Kingsolver and Virginia Henry Kingsolver. Her father spent a productive career as a physician in rural Kentucky, where Kingsolver as a child observed great discrepancies between rich and poor as well as nearly complete racial segregation. She valued the strength and vivid speech of the poor people she knew there, and she deeply loved the hills and woods surrounding her. However, she saw few opportunities for herself in Kentucky and left it as soon as possible, first for college at DePauw University in Greencastle, Indiana, and then to make her permanent home in Tucson, Arizona. She has traveled and lived abroad on several occasions, most importantly as a child in Africa with her parents, as a young adult in Europe, and more recently, in protest against the Gulf War, in the Canary Islands. She has married twice and has a daughter from each marriage. Her elder daughter, Camille, was born to her marriage to Joseph Hoffmann, a chemist and professor at the University of Arizona; that marriage ended in divorce in 1993. Her younger daughter, Lily, is the child of her marriage to Steven Hopp. She has worked at a variety of jobs, the most important being as a scientific and technical writer, as a journalist and freelance writer, and finally as a professional novelist. Her career as a novelist, thus far only about ten years long, includes the publication of four novels and four other books (poems, short stories, nonfiction). Her works, which tell the stories of vigorous and vital women in vivid and often poetic language and which are thematically responsive to many of the major issues of our day, have been well, even enthusiastically, received.

PERSONAL DETAILS

Although Kingsolver left Kentucky as soon as she could and although she speaks of many aspects of the rural culture she knew there in negative ways, she refers to Kentucky lovingly, and she is grateful for its influence upon her. In part, that influence was simply her close and loving family. Her parents were socially active and conscious people who lived to be of service, to be useful, and this strong value was impressed upon their three children. The writer has called herself "the fortunate child of medical and public-health workers" who lived with "compassion and curiosity" (*Poisonwood* x). Dr. Kingsolver, descended in part from Cherokees, was known to everyone in Nicholas County, Kentucky, and admired and respected for his medical services to the poor. Her father, she said later, "was an example to me in terms of doing what you think is right regardless of whether or not that's financially or otherwise regarded" (Farrell 29). Most dramatically, the senior Kingsolvers demonstrated to their children their commitment to helping others by working abroad when Barbara was quite young. They lived for a time in St. Lucia, in the Caribbean, as Dr. Kingsolver worked in a convent hospital, an experience which later inspired the setting and perhaps even the central character of the short story, "Jump-up Day." They then lived in Central Africa, where young Barbara learned what it meant to be a complete outsider. She told an interviewer, "The people in our village had not seen white kids. I had really long hair that I could sit on and people didn't think it was hair, because hair doesn't look like that, and they'd try to pull it off. . . . I got a real extreme look at what it's like to be a minority. It was an enormous adventure . . . at the age of seven" (Epstein 34). These experiences were much later to become a part of the basis for *The Poisonwood Bible*, her most ambitious novel.

The Kingsolver parents were book lovers, and they saw to it that their children were surrounded by books. Reading was an important part of the family life, and there was no television in the home for most of her upbringing. The small public and high school libraries of Nicholas County became havens to the future writer, as she read voraciously and widely. In an essay which pays tribute to a high school librarian, "How Mr. Dewey Saved My Life," she mentions having read and been impressed by such specific works as *Gone with the Wind* and *Martha Quest* and by such authors as William Saroyan and Edgar Allan Poe. But she did not restrict herself to fiction, also reading works on anatomy and physiology, interests she would make important use of later on. In reading so widely, Kingsolver discovered several things: that literature could enable her to live many lives besides her own and that language— words—has power and beauty. More specifically, in reading Doris Lessing's depiction of southern Africa's "colour bar," she was "jarred" into recognizing the racial segregation surrounding her in Kentucky (*High Tide* 51). She gives credit to her undirected reading for opening her mind, and she views with great alarm movements to censor or limit what young people may read, for it was the very unlimited nature of her reading that enabled her to discover the books that changed her, that enabled her to see her world truly.

Kingsolver's origins in rural Kentucky affected her in two principal ways, giving her a deep love for nature and an understanding of the hills and woods she grew up in and demonstrating to her the cruelty of a culture in which divisions by race or class are made. Even after living in the deserts of Arizona for years and accustoming her eyes to that— to her—alien landscape, she says she still is "listening for [the] meadowlarks" of Kentucky, not the "howl of coyotes" (*High Tide* 6). Like her character Taylor Greer, she had to learn how to look at this land and how to understand and value it, simply because of its drastic difference from the place which had formed her. Kingsolver's youthful wandering of the hollows of rural Kentucky and her deep understanding of them surely led to her need to understand the place to which she transplanted herself and also to her concern with place in her fiction. Her essay, "The Memory Place," included in *High Tide in Tucson*, movingly describes some of the places around Horse Lick Creek which remain in her memory from a childhood lived in Kentucky's wild places. Her concern for ecology, present in all her fiction, grows from her early experience.

Although Dr. Kingsolver's profession might have given the family middle-class status, young Barbara always identified with the children of the poor tobacco farmers who made up the majority of citizens of the county and who were looked down upon by those who lived in town. This identification with the poor and uneducated was to become a hallmark of her fiction. She points out that, as a tobacco farming area, the country was "deeply depressed" and filled with divisions between groups of people (Epstein 34). Most obviously, there were separations between races and between economic classes. Blacks and whites moved in different worlds, their distance from each other being illustrated in her story, "Rose-Johnny." Economic differences between merchants and farmers, with the merchant families having all the money, also permeated the community and are strikingly illustrated in the opening to *The Bean Trees*.

Kingsolver's high school reflected the stratification of town and county. The popular young people came from the merchant families, while the rural youngsters were outsiders. She has described their deprivations with a few telling details: "they didn't get to wash their hair every night because they didn't necessarily have hot water. They had to walk through mud to get to the school bus, so they had mud on their shoes" (Epstein 34). She identified with the latter group, as her family lived in the country, and her parents did not accept the value system of the merchant class with its emphasis on possessions. Her county had no public swimming pool, but in neighboring Lexington, home of many great thoroughbred horse breeders, there was a horse farm which had a pool for therapeutic use by the horses (Epstein 43), a contrast which made Kingsolver envy and hate the horses and which drove home to her the cruelty of contrasts between wealth and poverty. The future writer resented her lack of "superficial things" such as new clothes, but she eventually came to value the lessons she learned through these experiences (Epstein 34). She learned about class divisions first by living them and then, later, by reading Marx and other economic and social theorists.

Joined with her experience of being an alien in Africa and her growing awareness of class and race distinctions was young Kingsolver's feeling of being an outsider for personal reasons. She was a shy child, buried in her books and journals, in a time and place where others did not share her interests. She was also very tall, reaching five feet six inches by the time she was in sixth grade. In the manner common for tall young women, she felt self-conscious because of her height. She did not date until near the end of her Kentucky years, acquiring her first boyfriend at the age of seventeen, when she attended some summer classes at the University of Kentucky. Her sense of being an outsider and her sympathy with those who are different, not accepted or understood by others, are based in part on these youthful experiences.

Her identification with and understanding of the poor Kentucky farmers and their families also influenced the language of some of her most interesting characters. Taylor Greer, narrator of *The Bean Trees*, speaks with a distinctively rural Kentucky idiom and cadence, one learned by Kingsolver from her Kentucky youth and spoken by her until she consciously shed it as an adult living away from her roots. She values its vividness and originality, however, and conveys it authentically. She has commented that she feels "really blessed to have grown up in a place where that poetic language is used, where people say, 'I'll swan,' and 'He's ugly as a mud stick fence' " (Ross 287).

Kingsolver knew from her girlhood that she must leave Kentucky, for she saw few opportunities for a girl like herself there. Thus she chose to leave the state for her college education, selecting DePauw University, a small liberal arts college in Greencastle, Indiana. Greencastle is not terribly far from her Kentucky home, and southern Indiana, even up to and including the Greencastle area, bears some influences of early settlement from Kentucky. However, to her this was a different world. She discovered at DePauw other bookish young people like herself, and she luxuriated in the life of the mind that she found herself able to live there. She originally went to DePauw to study music, having won a music scholarship because of her training and ability as a classical pianist. However, after two years of studying piano performance, theory, and composition, she decided that music was not very practical. The concern for usefulness inherited from her parents urged her to go in a different direction. The interest in anatomy and physiology shown in some of her early reading led her to choose biology as her major. A major in English or in writing did not seem sufficiently practical, although she had been writing poems and stories since childhood, but she did minor in English and take a course in creative writing. Her discovery of poetry came while in college, and her impulse to write could not be stilled. She scribbled poems in the margins of her science textbooks. She graduated from DePauw, *magna cum laude*, in 1977.

It was during her DePauw years also that Kingsolver became something of a rebel. She adopted a distinctive mode of dress, which she much later described as including an army surplus overcoat, a green pith helmet, and army boots (*High Tide* 56). She also became involved in causes, demonstrating against American involvement in the war in Vietnam and forming liberal opinions on the hot issues of the day. In an open letter to her mother, written years later and apologizing for the pain she had caused her parents, she described the heady excitement of those years: "I had friends, lovers, poetry, freedom. I had opinions about abortion, Vietnam, the Problem that Has No Name [a reference to Betty Friedan's ground-breaking work of feminist theory, *The Feminine Mystique*]. I was reading Karl Marx and Betty Friedan" ("Untitled" 249). In fact, although the precise form some of her activities took may have pained her parents, she was following in the path on which they had set her by stressing the importance of a life that was lived by principles and for service.

When she was a nineteen-year-old college student, Kingsolver was the victim of what is now called "acquaintance rape," but for which at the time there was no special term nor the understanding that now exists of it and its effects on the victim. The event was traumatic and the memory would remain with her, as revealed in Kingsolver's later recounting the episode in an open letter to her mother. She had talked with her assailant in a bar and had a drink with him there. Flattered by his attention, she was pleased when he came to see her several evenings later, until he forced his way into her off-campus apartment and raped her ("Untitled" 256). She felt guilty, believing that she had somehow brought the rape upon herself and therefore deserved his brutal treatment. In her mind, she heard her mother saying to her, *"You met him in a bar. You see?"* ("Untitled" 256). She also felt guilty for having failed, despite her desperate efforts, to fight him off. Her reaction to her guilt and shame was to lie in bed, curled into a fetal position, trying to feel anger instead of simple desperation, a response typical of many victims of such an experience.

After DePauw, Kingsolver lived and traveled for two years in Europe. This was for her a time of freedom and experimentation, during which she worked at various jobs and observed ways of life different from those she had known in Kentucky and Indiana. For example, she lived in a commune in France for a time. The scenes she came to know and the people she observed have not appeared directly in her fiction. Difficulties with her work visa led to her return to the United States in the late 1970s, and on her return she traveled to Tucson, in search of a new and grown-up life, much as her creature Taylor Greer would later do in *The Bean Trees*.

In Tucson she, like Taylor, found a new community and new causes to support and work for. She enrolled in advanced graduate work in evolutionary biology and ecology, receiving a master of science degree in 1981 from the University of Arizona. She continued working toward a doctor of philosophy degree until she intentionally washed herself out of the program, feeling disillusioned with academic life, a disenchantment which she later described as a "crisis of faith" (Hile 75). In order to leave the program without embarrassment to herself or to her mentors, she invented an elaborate story about the desperate illness of a relative who required her presence. Her abilities as a storyteller came in handy in an unexpected way here, and she has later told this story as a joke on herself, wryly refusing to reveal the identity of the relative in question.

Her continuing and deep interests in biology and the natural world in general are revealed almost constantly in her writing by her uses of animal imagery and by her sensitive and accurate description of natural phenomena. Her scientific training also affects her writing more subtly by forming her process. She begins most writing projects with a question, much like a research scientist in the laboratory or in the field. Then she strives to answer that question, to follow it to all of its possible conclusions, so that just as the process of experimentation leads to the discovery of new learning for the scientist, her process of writing leads to new insights.

Upon leaving the doctoral program she became a scientific writer for the University of Arizona, managing for the first time to combine two of her great loves, science and writing. Her formal education ended at this point. Her self-education as a writer began, and she gradually started to think of herself as a writer. She eased into freelance journalistic work, which led most importantly to her reporting on the strike against the Phelps Dodge copper mining company in southern Arizona in 1983. Her first national publication, a brief article describing the strike and bearing the seeds of what was to become *Holding the Line*, co-written with Jill Barrett Fein and published in *The Progressive*, appeared in March 1984. This was the beginning of her professional career. At this point, the political activism she had practiced since her participation in antiwar protests while at DePauw merged with her life as a writer.

Her personal life centered around her marriage and motherhood, but the personal and the political can never be separated with Kingsolver. Married to Joseph Hoffmann in 1985 and the mother of Camille after 1987, she worked with her husband to build a home in the desert, moved with her then husband and daughter to Tenerife in the Canary Islands (Spain) in protest against the Gulf War, returned to the United States, and published in quick succession three novels, a book-length account of the strike which initiated her career, and collections of short stories, poetry, and essays.

These activities were punctuated by her divorce from Hoffmann and a period of life as a single mother. The divorce ended a marriage which had been presented to the world, most notably in an article in *Woman's Day*, February 18, 1992, as based on deep affection and respect as well as on hard work. Kingsolver had concluded the article with a statement of certainty that she and her husband were well fitted to each other: "I'm confident I don't need a new partner" (110). Three years after the *Woman's Day* defense of conventional marriage, Kingsolver published a piece in *Parenting* on the family, pointing out that unconventional families are varied and many and indicating that her daughter Camille had little discomfort with being the child of parents who were divorced (78). The divorce itself was very difficult for Kingsolver. She wrote later that "92 was a rotten year. My marriage of many years was transferred suddenly from intensive care to the autopsy table. I had long since come to terms with loneliness, but now I was also going to be single—something I hadn't been since age twenty-two" (*High Tide* 125). The problems and joys of being a single mother as well as an activist and writer now occupied her.

With success as a writer came opportunities to travel and to occupy herself in other ways. In 1993 she received a fellowship to serve as a visiting writer in a small college in Virginia. There she met Steven Hopp, an ornithologist and animal behaviorist faculty member who was to become her second husband in 1995 and father of her second daughter, Lily. The expanded family now divides its time between her Arizona and his Appalachia.

One unexpected and delayed result of Kingsolver's early training as a classical pianist may be seen in her participation, after she became an established writer, in a rock band, called the Rock Bottom Remainders.

With Kingsolver as the keyboardist, other members of the group were Amy Tan (vocalist), Dave Barry (lead guitar), and Stephen King (rhythm guitar). The group occasionally toured, its members having great fun with each other and playing for booksellers' conventions and the like, raising money for literacy programs. These experiences also gave her the starting point for an amusing essay, "Confessions of a Reluctant Rock Goddess," which appears in *High Tide in Tucson*.

PROFESSIONAL LIFE AND REPUTATION

Like several of her characters, Kingsolver has had a somewhat varied work history, although hers was rarely as undirected or aimless as that of Codi in *Animal Dreams* or as purely guided by necessity as that of Taylor in *The Bean Trees*. She did, however, give some of her work experiences to these characters. While in college she had earned money, she writes in "Life Without Go-Go Boots," by cleaning houses, setting type, and modeling for artists (*High Tide* 55). Her graduate school experience led her toward more directed and meaningful work, that as a scientific writer, which indirectly began her career. It led to her beginning to try some freelance journalistic work, and that led to the writing of her first written but second published book-length piece, her study of the 1983 strike of copper miners and their wives against the Phelps Dodge copper mining company. As previously mentioned, her coverage of the strike led to her first national publication in 1984. For this work, Kingsolver spent much time traveling the dusty side roads of southern Arizona and interviewing the women who became the focus of *Holding the Line: Women in the Great Arizona Mine Strike of 1983*. This experience taught her to compose longer pieces than the journalistic essays she had been selling. More important, it introduced her to the lives, the language, the concerns of the Mexican-American women whom she came to value and admire. And it taught her the importance of place in writing, an importance that is crucial to her fiction.

Kingsolver had kept a journal since the age of eight and wrote stories from her youth, although she never thought of these activities as anything more serious than hobbies. She wrote poetry while in college, but lacked the confidence to begin serious creative writing until much later. For this reason, her journalistic work is particularly important. She finally published her first work of fiction, a short story called "Rose-

Johnny," based on her recollections of an eccentric Kentucky woman, in *The Virginia Quarterly Review*, the first magazine to which she sent it, in the winter 1987 issue.

Her true career, as a writer of longer fiction began, in her version of it, almost accidentally. Pregnant with her first daughter, she was troubled with persistent insomnia. Her doctor suggested that she scrub grout in order to get through the long sleepless nights and to avoid rewarding herself for being awake, but she chose instead to closet herself—literally—and began to write the novel which became *The Bean Trees* (Perry 151). For this endeavor, begun secretly and not very seriously, she invented a character, Taylor Greer, who has some of Kingsolver's own background in rural Kentucky but lacks her education and sophistication. Taylor speaks with the Kentucky dialect Kingsolver consciously discarded while at DePauw, and she copies Kingsolver's journey from Kentucky to Arizona in search of a new home and opportunities. However, the likenesses between author and character do not extend much further than these somewhat superficial traits. Kingsolver claims that had her pregnancy not extended well past full term—Camille's birth was three weeks late—the novel would not have been completed.

On a momentous April Fool's Day in 1987, Kingsolver brought Camille home from the hospital and also received an enthusiastic letter from her agent, Frances Goldin, saying that the partial draft Kingsolver had sent her was so good that she wanted to auction it, an unheard of approach to selling the first novel of an unknown writer. As is often true of first novels, it is Kingsolver's most autobiographical piece of short fiction, and a number of its most important sources may be found in her own life and experience, transformed to make them appropriate for the particular characters she has created. One of the most obvious uses of autobiographical material is the trip in an old car—a Renault for Kingsolver, but the more plebeian Volkswagen for Taylor—from Kentucky to Arizona in search of a new life. Kingsolver also gave Taylor much of her own Kentucky background and many of her feelings about it. Additionally, Taylor's voice, the narrative voice of the novel, is much like that of Kingsolver herself before she consciously discarded that speech. Taylor has her creator's partly Cherokee ancestry as well as many of her attitudes. But there are also many differences, and Taylor is clearly an imaginatively created character. Kingsolver is an educated and cultivated woman, unlike her character, and the crucial events of Taylor's trip, her adoption of a new name and her acquisition of a small Cherokee child, are complete inventions. What Kingsolver has done is to take hints from her own experience and transform them into the kinds of adventures her character would be apt to have. The similarities between author and character are interesting, but they are not controlling.

The Bean Trees grew partly out of a short story called "The One to Get Away," partly out of another piece which Kingsolver thought of as the germ for a novel with which she had been struggling. She told an interviewer she had been imagining a place called "Roosevelt Park," which combined features of several neighborhoods and parks in Tucson which she knew well, areas which were "marginally poor," but this idea "just simmered for five or six years." Then she wrote a short story which told about the escape from Kentucky of a spunky but poor young woman who was similar to herself in some ways. A friend who saw the short story immediately commented that it should be the beginning of a novel, making Kingsolver look at it afresh. She then "realized that it probably was the beginning of my novel. I needed to bring in a character from the outside to look at this place with the same eyes that I was using" (Ross 287). The combination of Taylor's character and voice with the place she had imagined led to the creation of The Bean Trees, allowing her to reveal the sense of community she had found "in a place that more jaded folks would call bad real estate" (Ross 287), a community made up largely of women and children. In combining these motifs and in going back to the Kentucky idiom that had once been natural to her, Kingsolver found her own voice and created a successful novel which is humorous and serious at the same time.

The Bean Trees was published to an enthusiastic reception in 1988 and received an American Library Association award in that year. Like all her works, it has been kept continuously in print since then by HarperCollins. In an important review published in the The New York Times Book Review, Jack Butler praises the novel highly, saying that it "is as richly connected as a fine poem, but reads like realism." He praises the book's vivid language and use of scene, its characterization, and its complexity of theme and plotting. He raises some questions, however, about the way in which the novel works itself out, saying that it "lost immediacy for him" after a time, that Taylor was too perfect, always too correct in all her attitudes. He suggests that the "problem is one of over-manipulation," but he stressed that the novel is nevertheless a "remarkable, enjoyable book, one that contains more good writing than most successful careers" (Butler 15).

Other reviewers were equally enthusiastic, many of them without the doubts expressed by Butler. For example, Diane Manuel, writing in the

Christian Science Monitor, praises *The Bean Trees* as a "refreshingly perceptive first novel," and comments on its original language and rich character development (20). Margaret Randall's thoughtful review in the *Women's Review of Books* praises the novel as engrossing and "hilariously funny" (1). She notes its feminist awareness and strength, comments on its complex structure and theme, and remarks enthusiastically about its rich language (3). Karen Fitzgerald, for *Ms.* magazine, points out some of the novel's "ostensible contrivances of plot and character" and the dangers inherent in its "political correctness," one of the matters that had bothered Butler, but finds the novel "refreshingly free of cant" and calls it "vivid and engaging" (28). An anonymous reviewer for *The New Yorker* thought some of the prose "formulaic" but considers it an "easy book to enjoy" (102). Robert Mossman, for the *English Journal*, calls *The Bean Trees* "always engaging, heartwarming, poignant, surprising, and hopeful" (85).

Following the successful publication of *The Bean Trees*, *Holding the Line: Women in the Great Arizona Mine Strike of 1983* was issued in 1989 to less universal praise. The major issue related to Kingsolver's admitted lack of objectivity and her focus on the women involved to the exclusion, some reviewers felt, of the men, the actual strikers. Work on the book had begun, in 1984, close to the events it discusses, but the undertaking was put aside for some time because of difficulties finding a publisher. Finally, an academic press concentrating on materials in the field of labor and industrial relations accepted the manuscript. Kingsolver openly sides with the strikers, feeling from the beginning a kinship with them that rose from her progressive political beliefs. To her, the truly interesting aspects of the strike lay in the effects it had on women and families in the company towns which were engulfed in the events of the long and contentious strike as well as in the ways in which the women affected events. She combines straightforward reporting with novelistic techniques in her presentation of her materials. Thus it was perhaps not surprising that some reviewers wanted more factual data and more straight history of the strike, while others complained about her failure to give what they considered adequate representation to the activities of male strikers and her open partisanship. Kingsolver felt that some of these reviewers had overlooked the book's subtitle, and it might be argued that they were attempting to require her to write a very different book from the one she envisioned.

For example, Barbara L. Tischler, writing in *Labor Studies Journal*, defends Kingsolver's method of concentrating on the place of women in the strike and the lives these women led, including the difficulties they faced because of the preconceptions of their husbands and of the unions. However, she criticizes Kingsolver for not "providing a complete explanation of these obstacles and how they were resolved or left to fester until the next strike" and suggests that the author's partisanship with her subjects and consequent "tendency to fire verbal salvos at Phelps Dodge detracts from the power of her subjects' experiences" (83). Frieda Shoenberg Rozen, in *Library Journal*, largely agrees with Tischler, wishing for "fewer quotations and additional industry and strike background" (104). Page Stegner, whose review appears in the *The New York Times Book Review*, is particularly bothered by the concentration on women, appearing to have missed Kingsolver's sympathetic explanations for the reasons that men were largely absent: having been forced to go elsewhere in order to seek work, for there was no other employment in their strike-bound company towns, and unable to appear in large numbers on the picket lines because of legal limits on the numbers of union members allowed on the line at any one time.

Holding the Line is particularly important in Kingsolver's career for what it helped her learn about writing longer pieces. It taught her about place and its importance in giving a firm basis to a story, about listening and comprehending character, about letting characters tell their own stories, and about fitting all these elements together. It gave her materials she was to use with great effectiveness in novels, especially in *Animal Dreams*. It also increased her commitment to some of the causes and themes that would repeatedly appear in her later work. She told Jean Ross that she is complimented when people tell her that *Holding the Line* reads like a novel. She "wrote it scenically, and tried to be very visual and let the reader see the story as well as hear it through the voices of the women" (289). Thus techniques learned in the writing of this piece of nonfiction were to prove invaluable as Kingsolver invented herself as a novelist.

By now more confidently thinking of herself as a professional writer, Kingsolver turned to short fiction, practicing writing in a variety of voices and about a variety of themes and places. *Homeland and Other Stories*, published in 1989, won an American Library Association award in 1990. "Rose-Johnny," reprinted from its earlier appearance in *The Virginia Quarterly Review*, joins a number of newer pieces, mostly centered on women or girls and circling around themes of community and place, as indicated by the title story. This collection was favorably received, a number of reviewers commenting on its relationship to *The Bean Trees*.

Typical is Russell Banks of the *The New York Times Book Review*, who calls the stories "interesting" and says most were "extraordinarily fine," remarking also on the author's "Chekhovian tenderness toward her characters" and her "wise and female" humor (1). *Homeland* like *Holding the Line* may be seen as an exercise by the author practicing her craft before returning to her real love, the novel.

When *Animal Dreams* came out in 1990, it was greeted with delight as a new and different work by a promising writer now coming into her own. In this book, Kingsolver continues the attempts, begun in *Homeland*, to stretch herself as a artist. Taylor Greer's voice is so strong—so like her own—that the author intentionally moves to a very different set of characters and ways of telling the story, as well as to different, though in some ways related, themes. This novel won a PEN fiction prize and the Edward Abbey Ecofiction Award in 1991. Lisa See, writing for *Publishers Weekly*, comments that Kingsolver has "taken all of her previous themes—Native Americans, U.S. involvement in Nicaragua, environmental issues, parental relationships, women's taking charge of their own lives—tossed them into a literary pot and created a perfectly constructed novel" (47). Novelist Jane Smiley writes a thoughtful review for the *The New York Times Book Review* in which she comments on the difficulties writers face as they attempt "to forge a compelling political vision in our new world, where so many systems of social organization have turned out to be either ineffectual or bankrupt." Smiley suggests that Kingsolver tries to explore so many issues that she is only partly able to pull them together, but adds that she "demonstrates a special gift for the vivid evocation of landscape and of her characters' state of mind. That she . . . doesn't quite integrate everything into a perfect system, is probably to her credit" (2). David Keymer, for the *Library Journal*, calls the novel "upbeat but realistic" and says that the author's "dedication to complex social and environmental causes enriches the story line" (143). In addition to being greeted with largely favorable reviews, *Animal Dreams* was Kingsolver's first book to inspire significant scholarly attention, which focuses on the novel's use of place. Henry Aay, in 1994, published an article in the *Journal of Cultural Geography* on Kingsolver's use of environmental themes in the novel, also making use of Dan O'Brien's *In the Center of the Nation* for his study. Vicky Newman, in the following year, published in the *Peabody Journal of Education* an article on Kingsolver's use of landscape, community, and sense of place in *Animal Dreams*. The appearance of these articles signaled the seriousness with which Kingsolver's fiction was beginning to be taken.

Kingsolver's next publication was another change of pace. Her collection of poetry, *Another America/Otra America*, 1992, with its English and Spanish versions on facing pages, was published by a leading feminist small press, Seal Press of Seattle. This collection was, like the writer's prose work, generally favorably received, with reviewers commenting on the thematic connections between the poems and Kingsolver's fiction. The political consciousness of the poetry, particularly its concentration on connections with Latin Americans, whether in their original homes south of the U.S. borders or in the United States, was especially noted. Two brief reviews, both in the *Library Journal*, illustrate this point. Louis McKee praises Kingsolver for "never slipping into jargon and rant" despite the highly charged political and social nature of her themes and suggests that this collection reveals "just how essential poetry is to our lives." He highly recommends the book (92). Rochelle Ratner comments that the poems "make the tremendous leap from sympathy to identification, and they do so with craft and grace" (171).

With her next major publication, *Pigs in Heaven*, Kingsolver returned to Taylor Greer and her daughter Turtle, attempting not only to bring their story forward in time, but also to correct what she considers the serious error of seeming to condone not only the premise that a Native American child might be given away lightly, but also the notion that the welfare of the child is the only issue to be considered in adopting Native children out of their tribes. She does not, however, return to the direct use of Taylor's voice as narrator. Since this book continues the story of characters already familiar to the reader, it has to some degree a ready-made audience. HarperCollins gave this novel a first printing of 100,000, in contrast to the first printing of 25,000 for *Animal Dreams* and similarly increased the advertising and promotion budget for the novel from $30,000 to $100,000, according to *Publishers Weekly* (22 June 1990:45; 5 April 1993:62). These figures indicate her publisher's assessment of the increased sales potential Kingsolver's work was achieving.

The novel's critical reception was as generally favorable as had been that of the earlier novels. A British reviewer, writing in the *New Statesman*, comments that Kingsolver's "delicate balance between irony and tenderness . . . makes this novel a real treat" and suggests that she successfully avoids allowing the "heartwarmingly happy ending" from becoming "sentimental tosh" (Scott 40). Writing for the *Library Journal*, Marlene McCormack-Lee calls Kingsolver "an insightful writer" and concludes that "as Kingsolver brilliantly reveals from the first pages of this novel, the answers to our questions aren't delivered easily but must come from the heart," recommending the book for purchase for all general library collections (97). R. Z. Sheppard's review in *Time* is less wholeheartedly enthusiastic, suggesting that after setting up "a promising plot," Kingsolver "succumbs to her talent for winsome characterization," and summing up the novel's ending as a "nonconfrontational conclusion." Sheppard places this novel in a "middle ground between Tom Robbins's potty detachment and Louise Erdrich's righteous commitment to Native American causes," which allows her to create a "stylish romp" (65).

High Tide in Tucson: Essays from Now or Never, published in 1995, gathers together a number of articles, some revised, which have appeared in a variety of magazines and journals, along with three new pieces. Although these personal essays are inspired by their authors' experiences, they are more concerned with her musings on meanings than on the events themselves. Two of the new pieces, including the title essay, give a frame to the collection, which is loosely arranged in chronological order as the events and concerns they describe happen in Kingsolver's life. The third new piece, "Civil Disobedience at Breakfast," discusses her experience as a single mother and comments on some American assumptions about child rearing which she considers unfortunate. In so doing, it picks up important themes discussed elsewhere in the collection and forms a link between several of the essays. Although in this collection Kingsolver speaks more frankly and personally about her own life and experience than elsewhere, she succeeds in transforming her musings into more general significance, never remaining with the purely personal.

Like her fictional work, this collection was appealing to most reviewers. In *Booklist*, Donna Seaman writes of "relishing" the "vibrant self-portrait [in] these frank, bright, funny, and generous essays," calls them "[w]ry and to-the-point," and comments on the "great verve, honesty, and humor" with which Kingsolver approaches her varied themes (2–3). Paul Tractman, reviewing for *Smithsonian*, in which two of the essays, in different form, had originally appeared, stresses the language, calling it "transparent" but not at all "artless." He praises her uses of metaphor and what he calls a "kind of ferocity in her natural descriptions." Further, he points out her combination of the personal and the political and compliments her ability to see the "complexity of things" and avoid "the traps of self-indulgence and polemics" while maintaining "an undercurrent of humor" (24). Penny Stevens, in *School Library Journal*, praises Kingsolver as a "skilled observer of both people and nature" and indicates that she "presents . . . a vision of beliefs too often undervalued in our modern world" (134). Thus, language and theme make Kingsolver's essays appealing to both reviewers and readers.

Kingsolver's latest novel, *The Poisonwood Bible*, published in late 1998, is a striking departure from her earlier fiction in that it is set in Africa, far from Kingsolver's usual North American Southwest. It is a more complex narrative and is more serious in tone than the two novels about Taylor Greer and Turtle and *Animal Dreams*. A minor controversy about its publication erupted a year and a half before it was issued, when a news story in *Publishers Weekly* stated that HarperCollins had been forced to offer Kingsolver a particularly lucrative deal in order to remain as her publisher. According to *Publishers Weekly*, the reason Kingsolver considered moving was dissatisfaction with the booklist, which includes works by Newt Gingrich, maintained by the publishing house. The deal between Kingsolver and HarperCollins was said to include one million dollars as well as the establishment of a Bellwether Prize for Fiction recognizing "literature of social change." HarperCollins was to guarantee a first printing of 10,000 copies for the first winner of the prize, while Kingsolver was to fund the $25,000 prize from her advance for *The Poisonwood Bible* (Quinn 19). Kingsolver responded to the news story with a letter to the editor, saying that although the facts in the article were correct, she was not happy with being "cast as the grudging enfant terrible making Daddy Harper pay the price." She expresses gratitude to HarperCollins for standing by her over the years and never trying to "blunt the political edge of my work," and points out that while HarperCollins may publish "certain authors I'm not crazy about," it is also the publisher for a "gallery" of those with whom she is particularly happy to be associated. She named Doris Lessing, Isabel Allende, Milan Kundera, Louise Erdrich, and John Sayles ("Kingsolver Clarifies" 11).

With *The Poisonwood Bible*, Kingsolver clearly enters a new phase of her career, stretching her goals to the creation of a major and very complex novel which considers political issues of worldwide significance. In structure, narrative method, theme, and characterization, this newest book is the most ambitious work she has written as well as the book on which she has worked the longest, having begun wrestling with its materials as early as 1991. *The New York Times Magazine* treated the publication of *The Poisonwood Bible* as a major event: its first issue after the October 7, 1998 appearance of the novel on bookstore shelves included an article by Sarah Kerr on Kingsolver's life, work, and politics. Mostly enthusiastic reviews followed, with Michiko Kakutani, despite feeling that "social allegory" occasionally became a bit "heavy-handed," praising especially the characters of Leah and Adah Price and the author's use of detail. Kakutani concludes that the novel has a "fierce emotional undertow" (B43). In the cover review for *The New York Times Book Review*'s issue the week after the novel's publication, Verlyn Klinkenborg used such adjectives as "haunting" and "striking" to describe *The Poisonwood Bible*. It is clear that Kingsolver's reputation, hitherto most strongly based on *The Bean Trees* and *Pigs in Heaven*, will now be reassessed in the light of this latest, longest, and most powerful novel.

2

Politics and Genres

Although Kingsolver's reputation rests firmly on her work as a novelist, she has worked successfully in a number of other genres, including the essay, short fiction, journalistic reportage, and poetry. Her work in these genres reveals the same thematic concerns and the same care for craft as her long fiction and can be very illuminating as well as interesting to a reader of her novels. It might be remembered that she began as a technical and scientific writer, easing only gradually into the storytelling in which she found her true voice, and her work in other genres, especially her journalism as seen in *Holding the Line*, may be seen as preparation for her true work. The political concerns which fill all of her fiction, including her short stories, are also prominent in her essays and poetry.

Whatever her genre or theme, Kingsolver strives always to be accessible to her readers. Her political values and sympathy with all sorts of people are related to her literary goals. She wants her writings to be readable by the kind of people she writes about. She has frequently commented on her "serious commitment to accessibility. I don't believe that art is only for the highly educated. . . . I want to write books that anybody can read. I also want my books to be artful and as well crafted as I can make them: I don't want to offend educated people. I want to challenge people who like literature, to give them something for their trouble, without closing any doors to people who are less educated" (Ross 134). This commitment on Kingsolver's part leads her to create pieces which appear simply and directly told but which, when examined, are rich in complex construction and language.

Kingsolver shows great versatility in her fiction, using a variety of voices and technical methods to tell her stories and creating a range of believable characters. Equally, she shows versatility in the types of writing at which she has tried her hand. She feels at home in many genres. For her, as she told an interviewer, "there are some truths that are better told as fiction, and other truths that are most jarring and moving when you know they really did happen," as in *Holding the Line*. She added that "moments of light are often best revealed in a poem, or in a short story," and conversely that some themes work only in a novel because of the "weight" available in a longer work (Ross 289). But the themes which underlie her novels are generally the same as those which underlie her writing in other forms. In all genres, she strives to follow the goals she described in her essay, "The Spaces Between": "What seems right to me . . . is to represent the world I can see and touch as honestly as I know how, and when writing fiction, to use that variegated world as a matrix for the characters and conflicts I need to fathom" (*High Tide in Tucson* 154). No reading of this author can be complete which does not include a careful examination of her writings in poetry, short fiction, and nonfiction. As her thought is all of a piece, so is her creativity.

POLITICS

Politics in its broadest sense refers not simply to political parties and their competitions for power but rather to particular policies over which political parties or even governments may differ. Thus, we speak of the politics of the oppressed, or of those concerned about equality of races or peoples, or of the politics of the wealthy or powerful. For Kingsolver, political issues are and always have been important. The influence of her parents, with their need to be useful, early impelled her toward political views sympathetic to those who are poor or who are unjustly treated, for reasons that vary from race to economic condition to race or gender. These political sympathies have appeared particularly strongly in her fiction in several key areas: ecology, feminism, political activism on behalf of democratic movements in Central and South America, and concern for Native Americans and their cultures. All these concerns appear prominently in her fiction and connect her with so-called liberal movements of the 1980s and 1990s. Most recently, to these concerns she has added a concern for the native peoples of Africa. Anticolonialism, the opposition to the exploitation of the peoples of poor nations by wealthier Western nations such as the United States, links together her concern for the peoples of Latin America and of Africa.

Kingsolver's feminist and ecological themes are found throughout her fiction. In fact, they are so intricately woven into the fabric of her work that she has sometimes been referred to as an ecofeminist (Hile 77). All of her novels contain strong female characters, usually as the protagonists. When a female protagonist is initially a weak character, as is Codi Noline in *Animal Dreams*, a major motif of the novel is her gaining in strength and wisdom. In other novels, an important character such as Taylor Greer in *The Bean Trees* and later in *Pigs in Heaven* is resourceful and spunky, relying on her own common sense and wit, as well as on the strong friendships she builds, to overcome difficult obstacles. The women of the Price family in *The Poisonwood Bible* are the strength of the family and they finally win freedom, despite their early conventional subordination to their patriarchal husband and father.

Kingsolver is unhappy at having her novels labeled as "chick books," but only because she resents the assumption that important works must be about men. She told Donna Perry, "[M]y whole life I've been reading white guy books, and there's plenty of those in the world. And since I've never been a white guy, the most important stuff I have to write is going to be chick books" (159). She also has pointed out that "*Moby Dick* is a whale book, but I don't think only whales should read it" (Epstein 33). Literature, she thinks, enables readers to enter into the minds and souls of people unlike themselves; she believes her novels about women should not be of interest to women only.

The stories of Kingsolver's women connect them strongly to place, to the locales in which they find themselves, and for most of them nature is or becomes a teacher. Ecology, the relationship between human beings and the natural environment which nourishes them and which they often endanger by exploiting it and its resources, becomes a concern for these characters, either overtly or indirectly. In *Animal Dreams*, Codi Noline and her biology pupils discover that the river which gives the village of Grace its water is dying. It still contains larger fish but there are no longer any microscopic organisms; the larger living things nourished by them will inevitably also die off. This death of a river has been caused by the pollutants dumped into it by a copper mining company, much like the actual mining company whose actions Kingsolver observed as she prepared to write *Holding the Line*. She demonstrates in *Animal*

Dreams some of the potential results of such irresponsible actions toward the delicate balance of nature. The orchards which had given Grace much of its livelihood are dying because the waters which should bring life to them are instead bringing death. In attempting to avoid accepting responsibility for the results of its pollution of the river, the company is building a dam which, when completed, will flood Gracela Canyon and necessitate the removal of all its people and the destruction of their way of life. But, from the company's point of view, it will conceal the fact that the company has recklessly been destroying the ecology of the canyon all along. It is the anger of the women of Grace, strong feminists although they would not consider themselves such, that leads to the saving of the town and the defeat of the company.

Other novels show a similar concern for the land and its health, although they do not make this concern such an obvious theme. Taylor Greer, in both her novels, is sensitive to the beauty of nature, although her eyes must at first learn how to see the loveliness of the Arizona landscape, which is so different from what she had grown up with in rural Kentucky. Some of her most crucial experiences occur in natural settings, and her novels, both *The Bean Trees* which she narrates and *Pigs in Heaven* which she does not, are full of lovely natural descriptions. Similarly *The Poisonwood Bible*, set in a more exotic locale, the African Congo, powerfully depicts the response of the Price family to their new and shockingly different lush jungle surroundings. In all these books, the relationship between people and nature becomes centrally important.

Concern for the oppressed peoples of the world, another central political concern for Kingsolver, has shown itself in three principal ways. The destruction of the cultures of Native Americans in the United States was sometimes done with conscious intent. This is examined in Kingsolver's fiction through references to the removal of most of the Cherokees from the eastern United States to Oklahoma in *The Bean Trees* and *Pigs in Heaven*, a removal which is basic to much of what is shown about these people in the latter novel. The loss of a generation of young people, who were taken from their families to be sent to government boarding schools where they were not allowed to speak their native tongues and where white culture was forced upon them, forms an important part of the background of *Pigs in Heaven* and is less fully developed in *Animal Dreams*.

Sometimes, however, the destruction of Native American culture seems to occur, Kingsolver indicates, more by inadvertence than by intent, as in the giving of Indian children, who may indeed be orphaned and desperately need good homes, to well-meaning white couples who will not have the ability to teach the children about their birth cultures. Where the immediate good of the children may appear to call for such adoptions, Kingsolver argues in *Pigs in Heaven* that the adoptions are damaging to the welfare of tribes struggling to maintain their numbers and cultures and are often harmful in the long run to the children as well.

In two novels Kingsolver directly examines the effects of Western colonialism on what are now called "Third World" peoples, Central Americans in *The Bean Trees* and Africans in *The Poisonwood Bible*. In the first, she brings to Tucson several refugees from barbarism in Central America which is supported by the United States, and in the second, she takes an American missionary family to the Congo, where a corrupt government is supported by the United States after independence. In each case, she dramatizes the richness of the culture of some of the oppressed people and demonstrates that the Americans who pretend to be their betters are not necessarily such.

Kingsolver skillfully unites her abilities as a storyteller with her political concerns. She is very aware of the danger of preaching, and she works hard—and successfully—to make her themes and political points rise naturally from her plots and characters. Her slogan might be, "Don't preach," and she struggles to "refrain from diatribe" (Ross 286), which must not always be easy because of the passion with which she holds many of her convictions. She points out that the political novel is more accepted in many other countries than it is in the United States and is pleased and a bit surprised that her own work has been accepted despite her strong opinions. She told Epstein, "I think if artists can speak of things that matter, then they will be supported. I feel like I say stuff that people don't really want to hear. I write about child abuse, about sexism and illegal immigration laws, and I think, 'Nobody's going to read about this,' and yet they do. I think that you can say difficult things, but do it artfully, and you'll be heard" (36). She added that in general those who have attacked her work for being too political are people with opposing views, and she is in fact proud, not hurt, by that (Epstein 36). Kingsolver boldly claims to be a "pinko" who wants "to change the world" (Epstein 37).

Maureen Ryan, on the other hand, in a critical essay published in the *Journal of American Culture*, has attacked Kingsolver for not being political enough, in an ironic example of differences of opinion motivating negative evaluations. Ryan finds Kingsolver's happy endings to be evasions, suggesting that her characters unrealistically "recognize, grapple with, and finally overcome hazards large and small" (79). Kingsolver's solutions, Ryan suggests, lie in "the preservation of traditional values and time-honored customs" (79). She argues that Kingsolver evades "the big subjects, the looming dangers" (81) and finds Kingsolver's characters too good to be true. Kingsolver's message, Ryan concludes, is "seductive [and] seditious" (81), leaving readers unsatisfied. Basically, Ryan's argument with Kingsolver appears to be a disagreement with Kingsolver's view of the world, and her discomfort is with the persistent optimism that radicals like Kingsolver often feel. Their very convictions and activism imply that there is hope, that people can change, that the world can be changed, and that there can be happy endings.

GENRES

Journalism

Holding the Line: Women in the Great Arizona Mine Strike of 1983 was first published in 1989, after *The Bean Trees*, but had been written earlier. It is a complex study of a strike against a powerful mining company, focusing as the subtitle indicates on the involvement of women. It was issued by an academic press whose full name indicates its specialization in the field: ILR Press: New York State School of Industrial and Labor Relations, Cornell University. Kingsolver's concentration on women is crucial to any understanding of the book, and some early reviewers overlooked or refused to accept her approach. The other basic point to be made is that Kingsolver's approach does not pretend to be objective. She is clearly on the side of the strikers and against the mining company, and thus she practices an engaged journalism, not the more conventional sort of writing in which the writer tries to maintain the view of an unbiased outsider. Those critics and readers who faulted her for not emphasizing the male strikers or for not balancing the arguments of the mining company against the arguments of the union simply wanted her to write a different book than the one she had chosen to write, with totally different assumptions and goals.

Kingsolver herself was clear about both of these points. If the style and approach of the book itself had not made them sufficiently clear, her new "Introduction to the 1996 Printing" certainly does so. In that introduction, she summarizes her methods in preparing to write *Holding the*

Line: much time spent with the women of the towns in which the strike action occurred and many hours in interviews with the wives of the strikers and the other women, who for a variety of reasons became the people who actually carried on the strike itself and were the persons most affected by their experiences. She mentions a *New York Times* review which asked bluntly, "Where are the men?" The obvious answer, to Kingsolver and to the women who were the real subjects of the book, was, "That's just what we've been asking ourselves all this time. Where were the men?" (*Holding the Line* xv). She goes on to explain that for various practical reasons (this is made abundantly clear to any reasonably careful reader of the text of the book), most of the men were physically absent from the company towns in which the strike occurred. They needed to be elsewhere, working to support their families. Also, legal restrictions on the number of picketers who were union members caused the nonmember wives to take over that duty. "In truth," she says, "the men were present insofar as they were able to be" (xv). So Kingsolver's concentration on the women is not to be read as an intentional neglect of people who had been prime movers in the strike. Rather, it is both a recognition of the way in which events shaped people's actions and a choice made by a journalist of the focus which she found most interesting, namely, the effects of the women on the strike and the effects of the strike on the women.

Regarding the lack of objectivity of the writer, Kingsolver is unapologetic, and she offers her own background in explanation of the creative choices she made in this regard. She frankly admits that she began her investigations into the strike with sympathies for the situation of the strikers. Her background in rural Kentucky, she suggests, had taught her "the lessons of class struggle and the survival value of collective action" (xix). She had tried at first to maintain a conventional journalistic objectivity, but soon found this to be impossible. Because of the very placement of the strike in several small company towns in which everyone was well acquainted with everyone else, she stood out and quickly lost any anonymity she might initially have had. She could never have gained access to strikers and their families if they had not trusted her, and very soon the combination of her need to gain the trust of the people she wanted to write about and her natural sympathies thrust her firmly into the union camp. She calls her initial goal of maintaining objectivity an "absurd intention" with a short life (xix). Honesty compelled her to write a book which is not an unbiased account of a strike, following its history and political ramifications in some sort of logical structure. Instead, the book became a study of the women in several small communities and how they transformed themselves from conventionally self-effacing Mexican-American housewives to activists who are not afraid to take direct and confrontational action. These transformations become the real subject of the book.

As a result of these choices regarding subject and approach, *Holding the Line* does not accomplish some goals that many readers expect. For example, it puzzles by not including full historical information about the strike itself. The causes of the strike and the demands of both strikers and management are not clearly laid out, and readers may be left wondering just what all the fuss was about. Similarly, the results of the strike are not fully clarified. It is clear that the strike was not successful in that the men were not called back to work at higher wages or with increased benefits or job security. In fact, the results of the strike were disastrous for the continuation of the mining activity in these towns: Phelps Dodge closed down its mines. But in many ways, that seems to be beside the point—or at least beside what Kingsolver eventually discovered to be the point: the human impact of political action on women who had previously been almost completely apolitical.

Much of the book is taken up by reports of conversations held over coffee in the kitchens of the women of Clifton, Arizona, and several other small towns in which mines of the Phelps Dodge company were the major employer. Descriptions of the women and their family backgrounds and culture are carefully crafted, and the experiences of the women, along with their gradual emergence through anger to activism and even leadership, are related. This emphasis on these women and their growth and change clearly foreshadows much that was to be typical of Kingsolver's later fictional work. Most obvious is the fact that all of her work concentrates on women, with a decidedly feminist slant. Her protagonists and other important characters—Taylor Greer in *The Bean Trees* and *Pigs in Heaven*, Codi and Hallie Noline in *Animal Dreams*, and the women of the Price family in *The Poisonwood Bible*—are women, and these women are usually either strong to begin with or move toward increased autonomy as their stories progress. This movement toward greater self-awareness and power is typical, then, of the real women depicted in *Holding the Line* and is mirrored in the later women in Kingsolver's fiction.

More specifically, the women in *Holding the Line* come from the Mexican-American culture of the U.S. Southwest and live in remote villages. In this sense they are models for Emelina Domingos and the women of the Stitch and Bitch Club in *Animal Dreams*. Kingsolver became deeply fond of the women she met while covering the Phelps Dodge strike, and she came to know many of them quite intimately. Their experience of learning to comprehend the oppression being visited upon them by an uncaring and apparently monolithic company, supported by the power of the state, of learning anger at the treatment being given them and their families by this company, of finding in themselves the courage and other abilities to take the leadership in fighting that company, is very similar to the story of the women of Grace, as told in *Animal Dreams*. These stories differ in the origin of the struggle and in its conclusion, as well as in methods used by the women in fighting for their cause. In the actual story, the cause is a strike against the company, while in the fiction it is the discovery of the reckless actions of the company in polluting the waters and then attempting a cover up by building a dam which will force the removal of the people from Gracela Canyon. Further, in the actual story, the conclusion of the strike is decidedly mixed. In practical terms, the strikers lose, and what is gained is only the growth of the participants. In the fiction, the women win, and the dam will not be completed. The fictitious Grace will continue as a living community with a rich culture, but the real Clifton and other company towns have no such hope. Kingsolver's persistent optimism shows up in the denouements of her fiction, but her journalistic study could not reach such cheerful conclusions.

In her introduction to the reprinting of *Holding the Line*, Kingsolver points to two lessons from the story she has told. She sees the experience of the Phelps Dodge strikers as a "cautionary tale," with the lesson: "watch your back, America. Take civil liberty for granted at your own risk" (xxiii). If Americans do not learn from the experience of these workers and their families, similar events will continue to happen elsewhere. However, she sees the other lesson as being hopeful. These women, who began with low opinions of themselves and their abilities to affect events, did endure and even learned a "passion for justice instead of revenge," demonstrating that "ordinary people are better than they are generally thought to be" (xxiii). She emphasizes that she "did not invent these women; they invented themselves" (xxiii). In so doing, they gave her the materials with which she was able to invent the women of *Animal Dreams*.

Holding the Line is crucial to Kingsolver's career in another, more practical way. It is her first attempt at extended writing, in either fiction or nonfiction. At the time, she was a scientific writer and was beginning to do some journalistic freelance work. She won an assignment for work on the strike, which she at first saw only as another chance to earn some money through writing. However, as she drove repeatedly between the affected southern Arizona towns and began to know the people and the entrenched power, both economic and political, which they were facing, she began to see that a series of newspaper articles would not do justice to the information she was uncovering or the strong feelings she was finding within herself about the issues and people involved. She wrote a book "because I saw no other decent option" (xiii).

In writing a book, she learned that she could create longer, more complex, and more humane pieces than she had previously achieved. In so doing, she also practiced using many novelistic techniques: characterization, principally, but also narrating a story, keeping several related plot lines going simultaneously, building scenes, connecting interrelated themes, and uniting the whole into a unified structure. She herself sums up these elements as "lively characters, conflict, plot, resolution, even metaphor and imagery" and indicates that one publisher, in rejecting an early draft, said "We like this a lot but sorry, we don't publish novels" (xxii). Most important is the sense of place achieved in the journalistic study, which is also so central to the appeal of her fiction. She describes this as learning "to pay attention: to know the place where I lived" (xiv).

Short Fiction

After the publication of *Holding the Line*, her first foray into extended examination of a place and group of people, and *The Bean Trees*, her almost-accidental first novel, Kingsolver decided to turn her hand to another genre, that of the short story. Her goal was to gain more versatility, to practice using a variety of voices, to create characters and situations different from those she had already invented. *Holding the Line* is a study of actuality. *The Bean Trees*, while in no real sense autobiographical, makes use of some aspects of her own experience and uses a narrative voice much like the Kentucky idiom which had been Kingsolver's own. *Homeland and Other Stories*, published in 1989 and winner of the 1990 American Library Award, is a collection of twelve short stories which range in setting from her familiar Southwest and the Kentucky of her childhood, which had briefly appeared in her first novel, to the Indiana of her college years, to California, and to the island of St. Lucia in the Windward Islands. Kentucky is particularly important, serving as the setting for several of the stories. Although the settings are varied, the sharpness of focus on place is as strong as in this author's longer fiction. While including major themes familiar from Kingsolver's novels, themes, like settings, are more varied here. Some stories are closely related to materials used in other works, as, for instance, "Homeland" in its use of the Kentucky background and Cherokee ancestry given to Taylor Greer in *The Bean Trees* and "Why I Am a Danger to the Public," which deals with a copper-mining strike much like the one Kingsolver covered in *Holding the Line* and a spunky female protagonist like some of those she came to know and admire while working on that book. Kingsolver has called the story a "collection of things that didn't quite happen but could have, and I sort of wish had" (Ross 288).

The title story, "Homeland," establishes the central focus of these stories. An emphasis on place, what it means to characters and how it influences them in both positive and negative ways, is the unifying notion for the collection. In "Homeland," Gloria St. Clair tells her own story about a Kentucky girlhood. But her story is equally about her great-grandmother, whom she remembers as a very old woman, a Cherokee member of the Bird Clan and one of the Cherokees who escaped being taken west to Oklahoma on the Trail of Tears in the nineteenth century. These are familiar materials for readers of Kingsolver, taken from her own background and given to her protagonist Taylor Greer of *The Bean Trees* and *Pigs in Heaven*. In working with these materials in this story, Kingsolver has Gloria explain how she pieced together details about her Great Mam's life and personality. Particularly revealing is Great Mam's change of names: her Cherokee identity was taken from her. Gloria knows, although she doesn't seem sure how she knows, that Great Mam's original name was "Green Leaf," but her tombstone identifies her as "Ruth" (4). The dates of her birth and other crucial events are unknown and those in the printed records have been made up by her descendants. They gave her a Christian, a Western identity, erasing the truth of who she really was and replacing that truth with fabrications more comfortable to themselves. However, Great Mam, while she is alive, retains her old lore and some of her Cherokee customs. "You keep it stored away," she tells Gloria. "If it's important, your heart remembers" (6). Great Mam urges Gloria to tell her stories to her own children in order to keep the Cherokee world alive in her own descendants, and the existence of the story is evidence that Gloria's heart has remembered and that she later attempts to do as her great-grandmother had requested.

The principal action of the story involves a trip taken by Gloria's family enabling Great Mam, in what turns out to be her last year, to revisit her childhood places. They travel south to a town called "Cherokee," which is filled with what the tourists may accept as authentic Cherokee crafts and sights, but which Great Mam rejects as having nothing to do with her own people. She says she recognizes nothing and points out that Cherokees do not wear feather bonnets like the dancers in a parking lot. Her loneliness as an isolated member of her tribe is emphasized by the fact that Gloria, who realizes that some things she had expected because of her Great Mam's stories are missing, nevertheless can't quite imagine Indians without feathered headdresses. After a brief stop at Cherokee, the family returns home. The visit clearly was meaningless to Great Mam, and it taught the family nothing about their Native American heritage. The buffalo which they see at a roadside park is symbolic: a sign on the unkempt, half-blind animal's cage reads, "Last Remaining Buffalo East of the Mississippi" (18). Gloria thinks about how lonely it must be with no buffalo companions. She does not explicitly compare its plight with that of her great-grandmother, whose Cherokee relatives are also mostly west of the Mississippi, but she attempts to feed it some grass. Her brother, however, thoughtlessly throws gravel at it. If Great Mam had any reaction to this, it is not mentioned.

Great Mam accepts her isolation with courage. The description of the trip is immediately followed by two brief passages which tell contrasting creation myths. The first, in third-person narration, relates a Native American creation myth about a waterbug and the star people. In the second, a dialogue between Gloria and Great Mam, Gloria questions how the Cherokee tale can be true if the biblical story of Adam and Eve is authentic. With her usual composure, Great Mam claims that Adam and Eve were probably the children of the waterbug and that by bringing sin into the world they were only doing what children always do—cause great grief to their parents. But, she adds, parents have children anyway. "It all works out" (20). That last brief statement, along with "Remember this," seems to sum up her basic attitude toward life. Tolerantly she accepts the beliefs of others, but she insists on the validity of her own beliefs as well and does what she can to ensure that they will last at least one more generation.

The final paragraphs, describing Great Mam's burial, emphasize yet again the pathos of her situation, caught between two cultures and even at her death not allowed to be buried according to the customs she held dear. Yet Gloria feels the strength of the old ways. Great Mam is given a Christian burial, in the grave which will ultimately bear the name "Ruth" and which is decorated for the first and only time by flowers. But Gloria has a notion of another world nearby. "The small people" of her great-grandmother's Cherokee lore would, "as soon as we turned our backs,"

> come running and dancing and pick up the flowers. They would . . . run through the forest, swinging the hollow stems above their heads, scattering them like bones. (22)

Somehow, for Gloria, the force of her great-grandmother's personality and the beauty of the Cherokee world she inhabited are great enough to triumph spiritually. But just as the bones are scattered and Great Mam's body will decay, so too will the Cherokee lore be lost, except for Gloria's memory and retelling. Gloria is an outsider, not truly a Cherokee, so in her retelling her great-grandmother's world will be seen from the outside and perhaps even misunderstood, just as the tourist attractions of the town of Cherokee had falsified the Native American past. Kingsolver's story conveys the pathos of the situation of the last survivor of a culture as well as the clash of cultures suffered in such a situation. It also creates two wonderful characters in Gloria and Great Mam. Read in conjunction with *The Bean Trees*, it adds a dimension to the reader's understanding of the history and world of the Cherokee.

Three other stories are useful to show the variety and skill present in these stories. "Covered Bridges" is set in Indiana, not far from Greencastle, where Kingsolver's DePauw University is located. In this story, told by a mature and educated man—a very different voice from that most familiar in Kingsolver's work—a couple visits the Covered Bridge Festival, an accurately described annual autumn event in which Parke County, Indiana, plays host to tourists. The narrator and his wife seem to feel the ticking of their biological clocks and are considering having a child. Throughout most of the story, events and people seem conspiring to lead them to decide that they will not be a complete family unless Lena becomes pregnant and bears a child. But one dramatic event puts everything in perspective for them. Lena, who is allergic to bee venom, is stung, goes into anaphylactic shock, and nearly dies. She is saved by her own calmness in directing others in caring for her and by her caution in always carrying with her the antidote needed in such a case. Finally, after her release from the hospital, they agree that unlike most married couples, they do not need to have children in order to be complete. Each of them is the sum of what the other wants. The story is a convincing depiction of a solid marriage, of people who make rational decisions when emotion might otherwise easily override their sense, and an accurate and believable description of one of the great many festivals which dot the middle west during the summer months.

"Rose-Johnny," another Kentucky story making use of poor and uneducated people, is perhaps Kingsolver's best-known effort in short fiction. It was her first published short story, appearing in *The Virginia Quarterly Review* in 1987 and later reprinted in *Homeland*. It is unusual for Kingsolver in having been inspired by a character rather than by a question or theme (Ross 288). Like "Homeland" and *The Bean Trees*, it is told by a young Kentucky girl who lacks education but has courage and grit. This narrator, Georgeann Bowles, at ten and eleven over the course of the story, is younger than the others, and since she does not understand many events at the time they occur, she may be seen as a naive narrator. Since her understanding of events and people is partial because of her inexperience, the reader knows more than she does. The narrative centers around her curiosity about the title character, an eccentric and controversial inhabitant of her village, her relationship with Rose-Johnny, and finally revelations about Rose-Johnny's history which explain her odd behavior and appearance.

What is most obvious about Rose-Johnny, who keeps the village store owned by her father, Mr. Wall, is her mannish appearance. On her first encounter with Rose-Johnny, an errand into the store, Georgeann is frightened by the odd, even threatening, behavior of two men. They tell her not to come into the store again and return the quarter charged for her purchase. Puzzled, she asks her aunt, who as a first-grade teacher is the most educated member of the Bowles family, about it. Aunt Minnie, in the custom of elders trying to protect youngsters from unpleasant information or themselves from having to instruct them in unpleasant facts, tells her that Rose-Johnny is a "Lebanese" and that she will understand all about it when she is older (209). That Aunt Minnie is confusing two words, "Lesbian" and "Lebanese," is clear to the reader but not to Georgeann, who knows neither of these terms and is even more puzzled after she looks up "Lebanese" in a Bible dictionary, apparently the only reference work at hand. More confusion follows, but Georgeann establishes a relationship with Rose-Johnny as she begins working for her in the store, trading work for supplies. That this relationship is built on a lie to her parents bothers her, but not enough so that she confesses it.

Running parallel to the theme of Rose-Johnny's assumed lesbianism is her demonstrated concern for some African American children of the community. This is a strictly segregated town, in which the black youngsters must wait outside the store and come in to make their small purchases only after it is officially closed. Rose-Johnny is kind to the children, calls each of them by name, and insists that Georgeann also learn and use their names. Rose-Johnny, unlike the rest of the villagers, grants these children individual human dignity. Later, when Rose-Johnny is ill and Georgeann works alone in the store, she learns that Rose-Johnny had been charging the African American children much less than the listed prices. Not understanding the sexual politics of the village and its fear of homosexuality, Georgeann does comprehend something of the racial politics and realizes that there are complexities in Rose-Johnny's life that she does not understand. She also realizes that no one will tell her whatever the truth about Rose-Johnny may be.

The truth is revealed after Georgeann is in a fight at school because she defends Rose-Johnny from the cruel slurs of a schoolmate. A tragic and complicated tale of death and miscegenation (intermarriage between members of two different races) explains why Rose-Johnny has a particular affection for African Americans and a concern for children. It also explains her mannish haircut and her hyphenated name. Originally named Rose, she had been given the boy's haircut and the name of her little brother in order that she might be a living continuation of him, both Rose and Johnny. After this revelation, Rose-Johnny disappears, and Georgeann never learns whether she is dead or living somewhere else, as rumor has it.

But that is not the end of the story. Georgeann, who had lived a lie throughout her relationship with Rose-Johnny, is determined to tell all the truth she can about the enigmatic character and the effects of her own actions. Her sister is beaten up, and Georgeann is certain that she was the intended victim and that her connection with Rose-Johnny was the motivation. In pain and anger, she attempts to become more like Rose-Johnny, cutting off her hair and that of her doll to resemble Rose-Johnny's mannish cut and changing her name to George-Etta, so as to emphasize its combination of masculine and feminine parts and also to combine her own name with that of her sister, Mary Etta, who had been victimized in her stead. "Rose-Johnny" is a powerful and insightful story, and both Georgeann and Rose-Johnny are fully rounded, believable, and likeable characters.

A final story, worth special mention if only for its obvious differences in setting from the rest of Kingsolver's short fiction, is "Jump-up Day."

Set on the island of St. Lucia in the Windward Islands and again using a naive female narrator, this tale contrasts two very different belief systems, a theme also used in such other stories as "Homeland" and often in Kingsolver's novels. One belief system is the Catholicism of the convent school in which the protagonist, Jericha, is placed when her father, a doctor, returns to England to be healed of the schistosomiasis, an illness caused by a tropical parasite, which he has ironically contracted despite his careful precautions. The other is the indigenous *obeah* system, which includes belief in sorcery and originated in West Africa. Jericha's father had been an enemy of the practitioners of *obeah*, damaging the business— selling charms and potions—of one of them. This "Obeah Man," as he is called, involves Jericha in some of his magic, claiming that it is his sorcery which has sent her father away. His instructions to Jericha sometimes mix Catholic and non-Catholic elements, as when she is told she must attend Mass before participating in his sorcery and when he gives her what he calls a "Good Friday egg" and tells her to take it to Gro Maman, a deity in a tree. When they are doing sorcery and the Obeah Man sings in *patois*, the local dialect, Jericha creates her own spell, mixing the Latin of the Catholic Mass and a phrase originally from African folklore which she has learned from local people: " '*Hoc es corpus meum*,' Jericha sang very quietly, and 'Anansi he is a spider' " (199). The first, meaning, "This is my body," is the biblical phrase said by Christ and used by the priest in the sacred moment when bread is transformed into Christ's body. The second refers to a being important in much African lore. The two would seem to be incompatible, but in Jericha's mind, they have an odd equivalency. Whether the magic works is unclear, but Jericha does experience a kind of mystical moment at its climax. Afterwards, she frees Maximilian the goat, who had been intended to be their Easter meal and to whose fate she had previously been indifferent. No value judgments are made on the worth of the two competing systems, but their coexistence, sometimes uneasy, is dramatically revealed. Jericha's father, the outsider, seems to be the only one who is appalled at the native system. The system seems to have shown its power in that he is removed from the island before the story even begins. As is usual in Kingsolver's fiction, vital and interesting characters are created, most notably Jericha, a tomboyishly appealing rebel, and the partly ominous and partly fatherly Obeah Man.

Poetry

Kingsolver's one book of poems is both unusual as a collection of poetry and pretty much what might have been expected from this author. It is unusual in that each poem by Kingsolver, written in English, is accompanied on the facing page by a translation into Spanish. The poems' Spanish translations, by Rebeca Cartes, are given as much prominence as the English originals within the volume, and Cartes's name is prominently displayed, although in smaller type, below the title on both cover and title page (Kingsolver's name appears above the title in both places). The full title of the collection also emphasizes its bilingual character: *Another America/Otra America*. The publisher, Seal Press of Seattle, is an important feminist press which is also very progressive racially and politically.

It is in her poems and essays that Kingsolver most openly reveals intimate details of her life and beliefs. The poems strikingly connect the personal and the political. The title refers to two Americas, but there is some ambiguity about the precise identification of the second, although the relationship between the two seems to be based primarily on language. The first America is that of the white upper class, those who would most often be assumed to be the readers of poetry as well as those forming the majority opinion of the nation. The second America is, in part, that America living in poverty and economic, racial, or sexist oppression. A number of the poems support this interpretation. "What the Janitor Heard in the Elevator," a conversation between two women about firing a maid who had broken a vase (5), is based on the irony of the women's insensitivity not only in seeing the maid as an object less important than the vase she is accused of having carelessly broken, but in being so self-assured and self-centered that they speak openly of the treatment they assume she merits in front of a janitor, like the maid a domestic worker, as if he or she had no ears to hear and no feelings to anger. Although the vase was important because, as the woman laden with expensive jewelry explains, it went with her decorating style perfectly, she is already planning to replace it with an identical one. Ironically then, the vase is not even distinguished by being one of a kind; it is easily replaceable. Unspoken but assumed is the fact that the maid, less important than the vase, is also not one of a kind and is also easily replaceable. The women smugly assume that the money which gives them power over people like the maid and the janitor also gives them the right to dehumanize the powerless. The class system based on economics leads to those in powerful situations being unthinkingly cruel and having no notion that their behavior is in any way unworthy.

However, there is more to "What the Janitor Heard in the Elevator" than its depiction of the smug brutality of two upper-class women. Racial—or at least linguistic—politics are also present. After the first longer verse paragraph of eleven short lines, two brief verse paragraphs, which total five lines in length, introduce the matter of language. The friend advises the first woman to hire somebody else who speaks English. Maids and janitors are not all exactly alike. Distinguished by language, those who do not speak English but presumably only Spanish, are less human, less worthy, than others. Within the economic class of those who must do menial labor for people like the jewelry-bedecked woman there are gradations of worthiness. No hint is given whether the janitor is Hispanic or not, so a reaction to the prejudice against nonnative speakers is not indicated. In fact, the janitor's presence is revealed only by the title, emphasizing even more strongly his or her absence from the world of the wealthy women. They are not even aware of the janitor's presence, or if they are, do not see him or her as being sufficiently important to make them alter their thoughtless conversation—they assume the janitor will not understand it. The janitor is as dehumanized by their lack of concern for other's feelings as the maid is. Despite the richness and complexity of this short poem, Kingsolver disclaims credit, saying it is "an exact transcription of a conversation" she overheard and then wrote down (Perry 164).

The language theme, introduced in the final five lines of this brief poem, identifies the second interpretation of that "other America": the Spanish-speaking peoples of the Southwest United States and of Central and South America. This theme reminds readers of the presence of a vital Spanish-speaking community in the Southwest, the ancestors of many of whom were in this area before English-speaking settlers arrived. Many others are current immigrants, some fleeing from political or economic oppression in their homelands, hoping to find political freedom or economic security here but too often being welcomed by more oppression or by being imprisoned and then forcibly returned to their homelands. These are themes crucial to Kingsolver's fiction as well as to the collection of poems. *The Bean Trees*, with its important subplot about political refugees from Guatemala and its loving characterizations of Estevan and Esperanza, contains some of the most direct uses of refugee materials. *Animal Dreams*, in depicting the mainly Mexican-American town of Grace, settled in part by immigrants who came directly from Spain, is a reminder that not all Hispanics in the Southwest are wetbacks (illegal immigrants from Mexico, crossing the border by stealth to find employment in the United States). The "other America" of Kingsolver's poems, then, refers to the poor or to those of Spanish-speaking origins—or, more usually, to both.

The collection is divided into five sections, each with five to nine poems. The titles of the sections suggest a logical arrangement. The first section is subtitled in English, "The House Divided," setting up the notion of the two Americas, a theme, according to Kingsolver, of "alienation, how far from each other we are" (Perry 164). "What the Janitor Heard in the Elevator" is, appropriately, one of the poems in this section. The other four sections suggest by their titles some of the sorts of people who are part of the "other America", including "The Visitors" (in Kingsolver's definition, "people who have come here"), "The Lost" ("people who have been hurt badly by this alienation"), "The Believers" ("people who have saved themselves from being lost by believing in spirituality or love or family or something that gave them a path out of the woods"), and "The Patriots" ("political activists who have reclaimed that word") (Perry 164). Despite the increasing hopefulness indicated by Kingsolver's descriptions of the sections, all parts of the collection are filled with pain.

Since Kingsolver speaks in these poems, often in her own voice, of many of the concerns which underlie her novels, a brief examination of several sections in this collection makes a good introduction to her world and attitudes. The first section, "The House Divided," may be characterized by "What the Janitor Heard in the Elevator" but also contains other subject matter and themes. The first poem in the section, which sets the tone for the collection as a whole, is called "Deadline," dated January 15, 1991. It refers to the Gulf War of that year, fought in the Middle East, ostensibly to keep Iraq from invading and annexing Kuwait, a war which had wide popular support among U.S. citizens. Other poems speak of sexual and gender discrimination. For example, "Reveille" speaks for women who undergo cosmetic alterations so as to suit society's assumptions about what is beautiful. The examples range from the use of deodorants and perfumes, which destroy natural odors and mask them with unnatural scents, to Oriental women who curl their straight hair and African women who straighten theirs, all so they will be more acceptable in a land in which the primary ideal of beauty is of European origins. "Street Scenes" evokes the experiences most women have had of being harassed on the streets; in one example, two women are accused of being lesbians, in another they are vulgarly discussed as sexual objects by a man. In this poem, the speaker does show an appropriate anger, and the result, in the final section of the poem, is that she routs another tormentor.

The second section title, "The Visitors," is highly ironic as the first poem, "Refuge," makes clear. The poem is dedicated to a woman who has been raped and deported by immigration officers. The irony is that the United States, which in the nineteenth century claimed to be open and welcoming to immigrants, mainly from Europe, of course, now not only rejects a new immigration from Spanish-speaking America, but adds to the pain of the newcomers through brutal and inhumane treatment. Another irony, and another broadening of the collection's interpretation of its "other America," is presented in "For Sacco and Vanzetti." This poem grieves for the two anarchists, one a shoemaker and the other a fish peddler, convicted in 1927 because of their radical politics of a murder which they almost certainly did not commit. The poem also mentions the Rosenbergs, convicted of spying for the Soviet Union in the Cold War following World War II, in a highly controversial trial. The ultimate execution of these probably innocent people, killed in the view of many historians and scholars—not just poets like Kingsolver—for their political beliefs rather than for crimes actually committed, also broadens and adds to the definition of the "other America"—by now it has become all the downtrodden. Yet another poem in this section, called "In Exile," is dedicated to Rebeca, a refugee from Chile after the revolution which overthrew the legally elected Allende government and presumably the translator of these poems.

After two intervening sections, "The Lost" and "The Believers," which are filled with expressions of pain for lost lives, the final section is called "The Patriots." Pain is still a very important note here, but the anger, strongly implied but sometimes muted in earlier sections, achieves clear expression in this section. The section's opening poem, "On the Morning I Discovered My Phone Was Tapped," voices appropriate dismay at this invasion of privacy, compares the use of technology for listening to intimate conversations with the uses of telephone wires in torturing political prisoners abroad, and examines the psychological effect of realizing one's inmost thoughts may be known by others. Finally, the speaker refuses to allow her actions to be changed by the implicit threat of the wire tapping. A footnote summarizes groundless investigations within the United States in the 1980s of members of human rights organizations. The poem ends on a note of rebellion.

"In the City Ringed with Giants" makes use of some of the same materials discussed in the essay, "In the Belly of the Beast," which quotes the poem. The "giants" or "Titans" are the missiles placed underground to defend some U.S. cities from Soviet Union missiles during the Cold War. Visiting the underground emplacement of the missiles, Kingsolver is inspired to compare the humans who built and set them there to fish which live in dark caves and have lost the sight they no longer need. She observes that while we have outlived the missiles no longer needed now that the Cold War has ended, we have become blinded to humanity, having felt it necessary to establish such machines of war against our fellow human beings.

In "The Blood Returns," a succession of brief verse paragraphs speaks of episodes relating to war, torture, and killing. The fourth and final paragraph describes the training, in Georgia, of soldiers from Spanish America to return to their homelands to fight. Kingsolver does not specify here—she does not need to—that the training is done by the CIA or organizations subsidized by the CIA, and that the trainees will fight for right-wing revolutions or governments. Filled with strong images and sharp contrasts between beauty and pain, the poem is a powerful statement about the involvement of the United States in the internal affairs of Central and South American nations and the effect of such activity upon this country.

The last two poems of the book are personal statements, loving expressions directed toward special women. In both cases the women have undergone unspeakable pain, but the final poem ends on a note of hope. It is dedicated to Maura and Lesbia Lopez and spoken to Maura, describing the suffering of her mother, Lesbia. As a young girl, she was imprisoned, tortured, and raped. Maura is the child of this rape, and the poem ends noting Maura's resemblance to her mother. Out of great suffering has come something good. Lesbia has triumphed—Maura is *her* daughter, showing no inheritance from her anonymous and brutal biological father.

Another America/Otra America is a varied collection. It contains portraits of a variety of people and approaches its central theme, that of several Americas warring against each other, from a variety of directions. In so doing it achieves a complexity of ideas only hinted at by the title. However, the poems are also unified in technique, written in free verse with short lines and mostly short verse paragraphs, and the poems themselves are often brief. Their brevity adds to their power, for many poems rely on a particular sharp image or strong contrast to drive their message home. Politically their stance is clearly on the side of the oppressed, of the "other" Americans who are treated cruelly by the U.S. government or the established power structure. As in *Holding the Line*, Kingsolver makes no apology for her leftist and feminist stances, but she has no need to do so, as the collection of poems cannot be mistaken for being anything but a very personal statement. The poems, because of their very open statements about the political and other ideas underlying all of Kingsolver's writing, both illuminate and are illuminated by her fiction and other writings.

The Essay

Having begun as a freelance journalist and continuing as a reviewer and occasional columnist for magazines, Kingsolver has throughout her career busied herself with a variety of nonfiction prose work. In 1995 a collection of pieces, mostly reworked from earlier publication in magazines, was issued as *High Tide in Tucson: Essays from Now or Never*. Like her poetry the essays tend to make more use of autobiographical and personal details than her fiction does. The essays are varied in subject matter and in tone, but an underlying seriousness belies the humorous surface of much of the prose. Kingsolver takes on a number of profoundly serious subjects: U.S. missiles directed at the Soviet Union during the Cold War and remaining in place as reminders of the threat of mindless war in "In the Belly of the Beast"; the rhythms of life and fears and dangers (rape, miscarriage, death) that beset the unwary in the title essay; motherhood in several essays; self-exile as a response to the Gulf War in "Paradise Lost" and "Jabberwocky"; colonialism in Africa in "The Vibrations of Djoogbe"; and the place of violence in art in "Careful What You Let in the Door." More comic, for example, is her narrative of being a member of a rock band made up of well-known writers in "Confessions of a Reluctant Rock Goddess." In between lies a book review transformed into an essay about delight in natural transformations, "The Forest in the Seeds." These essays spell out more directly than the fiction, and in Kingsolver's own voice, the political views and concerns that are also present in her fiction. Thus like her poems, her essays are useful introductions to much of her thought and can serve to illuminate her fiction.

The essays' relative openness about personal matters, can also help the reader to know Barbara Kingsolver the person who strongly holds liberal political views, who considers herself an activist, who wants to be useful, who fervently treasures her motherhood of a much-loved daughter, and who feels deeply rooted in two places—the Kentucky of her girlhood and the Arizona of her adult life. The alert reader can find in the essays traces of the personal experiences and observations which Kingsolver has given to her characters. Her sharp wit and good humor, her persistent optimism despite all the evils she sees about her, are present everywhere.

Although the collection does not pretend to be a unified series of essays, it does have a carefully considered sequence, in which some essays are tied thematically to those which precede or follow. Kingsolver also gives the collection a certain unity by creating a frame for it. In the final brief "Reprise," written specifically for this purpose, she picks up the central image of the opening—and title—essay: a hermit crab transported from the ocean to dry Tucson, who teaches her that there are tidal rhythms even in arid locations which can symbolize the rhythms of our lives.

That title essay ranges broadly over typical life experiences, listing some of the most painful events of Kingsolver's own life and asserting that one thing she has learned is joy: "I have taught myself joy, over and over again" (15) she claims, adding that "To be hopeful, to embrace one possibility after another—that is surely the basic instinct" (16). Despite a number of traumatic experiences including her transplantation from the green and hilly woodlands of Kentucky, which nourished her soul, to the aridity of Arizona, which she had to struggle to understand, she has, like Buster the transplanted hermit crab, learned to accept the rhythms of her life and to rejoice in them. She does not say that these lessons were easily learned, nor does she suggest that they must be true for others. But they are lessons that pervade much of her fiction, and they suggest what her answer would be to Maureen Ryan's criticism that her fiction is empty and unsatisfying because it finds reasons for optimism.

These essays fall squarely into the genre of the personal essay. That is, they are not meant to inform but to communicate the musings of their author on particular, often very personal subjects. They are intended to convey a particular notion of the world from a particular and perhaps special viewpoint. These essays convey the attitudes, experiences, and beliefs of a woman who is at once a novelist, a mother, a political activist, a sensitive observer of nature with scientific training, and a person of deeply held moral and ethical standards. In revealing the orator behind the voices of her novels, the essays introduce a wise and sensitive woman, and they are equally richly rewarding in themselves. With her typically self-deprecating humor, Kingsolver has said she resisted calling the book, "*Barbara the Marxist Takes on Life*, but that's what it is" (Epstein 36). It is also much more than that.

3

The Bean Trees
(1988)

Kingsolver has said that each of her novels begins with some question, not—as many readers have thought—with either some autobiographical experience or some character. For *The Bean Trees* that question concerned the ways in which people help each other come through great difficulties (Fleischner 20). The answers to that question are varied, some obvious and some subtle, as Kingsolver describes, "sometimes hidden and underground" (Fleischner 20). Friendships and community suffuse this novel. Taylor Greer, the novel's central character, has a gift for friendship, and she not only creates friends wherever she goes, but she becomes a member of existing communities of friends. Through portraying Taylor and the many people who become her friends, Kingsolver examines how friendships may be built and how much they mean. She demonstrates how the concern for others that leads to the development of deep friendships may also lead to political concern and involvement in political causes.

In fact, Kingsolver considers herself a political novelist (Perry 154–55), and her concern for politics reveals itself in a variety of ways. "Politics" in this usage refers to power relationships between people and to struggles over ideas and policies. The political novel, popular and respected in many other countries, is, as Kingsolver has often pointed out, not in high esteem in the United States. When an interviewer asked if she objected to *The Bean Trees* being called "a political book" or herself "a political writer," she responded, "Of course not. . . . I'm only going to write a book if it's addressing subjects I care about. It surprises me constantly that almost everybody else in the United States of America who writes books hates to be called a political writer. As if that demeans them" (Perry 154). Thus, despite the novel's origins as a distraction during the sleepless nights of Kingsolver's first pregnancy, it touches on issues that are deeply important to her. She not only accepts the accusation of being a political writer—a writer about ideas—she takes great pride in that reputation.

PLOT DEVELOPMENT AND NARRATIVE METHOD

The basic plot of *The Bean Trees* follows the travels of Taylor (formerly Marietta) Greer. A brief synopsis shows that these travels take her first from her girlhood home in Pittman, Kentucky, westward through Illinois where she selects her new first name and Oklahoma where baby Turtle is thrust upon her, to Tucson, Arizona. There she finds friends and establishes a new home, only to set out on a journey back to Oklahoma in order to regularize her relationship with Turtle through legal adoption. Along the way, she has a variety of adventures, meets people of varied races and moral values, and learns about evil in the world.

The plot is much more complex than the above summary suggests. Several subplots interconnect with Taylor's story, each concerning important and rounded characters with their own backgrounds and experiences. Most important of these are Lou Ann Ruiz, who becomes Taylor's closest friend, housemate, and companion in child rearing, and Estevan and Esperanza, Guatemalan refugees who must come to terms with their own private torments as they seek a safe haven in the United States.

The story is told mostly in a first-person narrative. However, early in the novel, first-person chapters told by Taylor alternate with chapters told in third-person narrative focusing on Lou Ann. The first, third, and fifth chapters cover Taylor's background and childhood in Kentucky, her journey through Oklahoma to Arizona, her acquiring Turtle, and her early days in Tucson. Meanwhile, the second and fourth chapters introduce Lou Ann's background history and prepare the reader for the narrative combining the stories of Taylor and Lou Ann. These two characters meet in the fifth chapter when Taylor agrees to move in with Lou Ann. From that point on, Taylor narrates their adventures with Lou Ann as a principal secondary character.

The subplot surrounding Lou Ann is simple and lacks much action, being primarily concerned with her internal growth and her need to make decisions about her failed marriage. It concludes with a more mature Lou Ann accepting the end of her marriage and now ready to face an independent life. The subplot surrounding Estevan and Esperanza is more complex, and parts of their story are revealed only gradually as Taylor learns about their tormented pasts and thus is able to better understand their behavior, sometimes strange to her, in the present. The loss of their child, kidnapped from them by political enemies, and their intimate knowledge of torture methods used by the Guatemalan police, as well as their familiarity with sudden death by ambush have made it difficult for them to trust others. Esperanza especially is still deeply depressed and disturbed by what has happened to her. It is through their friendship with Taylor and other characters that they regain some degree of emotional health. Finally, in a climactic scene, they are able to risk detection as illegal immigrants, which could lead to being forcibly returned to Guatemala—and then to death—in order to help Taylor adopt Turtle. That brave and sacrificial act of love concludes their subplot and they disappear from the novel—and Taylor's life—immediately after it.

The plot is neatly concluded, with all loose ends tied up as the novel ends. Far from the Mexican border where they are most in danger of detection by immigration authorities, Estevan and Esperanza have found sanctuary with a church group in Oklahoma, near an Indian reservation where their Mayan features allow them to appear to fit in. Taylor has official papers which show Turtle to be her legally adopted daughter, and the two of them are preparing to return to Tucson to their new life. Lou Ann has given up on her marriage and is happily seeing a new man while eagerly waiting for Taylor to return. Even Taylor's mother, offstage throughout most of the book, is beginning a new life and marriage in Kentucky. A happy ending, restoring order to the world of Kingsolver's characters, seems to have been achieved. (However, readers of Kingsolver's third novel, *Pigs in Heaven*, learn that this is only a temporary respite for Taylor, Turtle, and Taylor's mother.)

CHARACTER DEVELOPMENT

The protagonist and principal narrator of *The Bean Trees*, Taylor Greer, is a striking young woman, a strong character who usually knows what she wants and what she wants to do and goes about getting and doing it. She is also a sympathetic and ethical character, honest with others and with herself. She is confident that she can do whatever she sets out to do. The exception is during a period of depression near the end of the novel when she doubts her ability to be a good mother to Turtle and her right to keep Turtle with her. She is practical, and her view of the world and of life is almost always realistic.

Taylor is also a natural friend and a builder of friendships. Wherever she goes, she demonstrates that she is one of those proverbial persons who never meets a stranger. This gift explains why she is seldom alone. Because she is natural, outgoing, and concerned for others, people spring to her assistance when she needs help. Broke and with a nonfunctioning car while on the road, she finds a motel whose manager is not only willing to take her in but provides her with employment until she gets her car fixed and is able to continue her journey. In Tucson, she finds work several times because her friendliness to strangers encourages them to trust her and see in her the makings of a good employee. Answering a newspaper ad for a roommate and establishing immediate rapport with Lou Ann, the woman who had placed the ad, leads very quickly to friendship. Their recognition of each other as displaced Kentuckians helps create their quick liking, but it is Taylor's (and Lou Ann's) innate qualities which make their friendship not only quick to grow but deep as well.

Taylor's solid character and self-assurance come from her early life in Kentucky. She is the daughter of a woman almost as indomitable as herself and a father who had long ago deserted his family. Her mother, whom she refers to as "Mama" in this novel, plays only a minor part here but becomes crucial in *Pigs in Heaven*. Nevertheless, Mama's important influence on making Taylor a strong and independent woman is clear. Mama always encouraged her and acted as if her every accomplishment were wonderful. Mama cleaned other women's houses and took in laundry in order to support herself and her daughter. When Taylor leaves Kentucky to strike out on her own, she is not rejecting her mother, and they keep in touch by telephone and postcard. However, they are physically separated from almost the beginning of the novel, and Mama's influence is felt through Taylor's thoughts about her and their occasional correspondence and telephone conversations. Mama's presence is especially strongly felt near the book's end in an important telephone call in which Taylor spills out her feelings about her impossible love for Estevan and her success in adopting Turtle. Taylor's love for her mother and her mother's practical and loving presence and influence thus frame the novel.

As a high school girl, Taylor had been deeply aware of the class divisions in her community, partly as a result of her mother's example and situation. Taylor always feels herself to be something of an outsider. She sees little hope for herself in Kentucky and is passionately determined to avoid the future that seems most likely, as it is the fate of most of her female classmates: early pregnancy, marriage, motherhood, and continued hard work for little reward—being caught permanently in the poverty and bleak life typical of Pittman, Kentucky. After high school she works as a lab assistant, learning to analyze blood and urine specimens and earning enough money to buy a decrepit Volkswagen. Her escape, even though it means leaving the mother who loves her and whom she in turn loves and admires, is earned and is a flight to a better life, even though she doesn't really know what that life will be. At least it will be different, and it will be on her own terms.

Her name change is symbolic. She had been named Marietta but nicknamed Missy. It was clear early on that "Marietta" was too frilly and feminine a name for the sassy and independent creature she became. She was never comfortable with it but didn't know what she really should be named. In the end she leaves it to chance and her gas tank: when the gas in her car runs out in Taylorville, Illinois, she accepts Taylor as her new name and the indication of her new identity as a separate and independent woman on her own.

Taylor rarely fears accepting a challenge. Even when a Native American baby is thrust upon her in Oklahoma, she has little doubt of her ability to cope. As usual, she simply goes on about her life, trying to do the best she can. She talks to the baby and cares for it, despite her lack of experience with children and her long history of taking great pains not to become pregnant. Ironically, she has found motherhood by fleeing from it. But she accepts this new responsibility with good humor, her concern for the child quickly outweighing any inconvenience it may cause her. She soon comes to love the child; by the end of the novel she is fighting to ensure that they will not be separated. The child's presence changes her life in some practical ways, for it requires that she be able to feed and care for Turtle, providing appropriate medical and other attention. She realizes quickly that the child has been abused, and her horror at the mistreatment of such a helpless being makes her even more determined to care for the baby and help it recover from the effects of its early life.

In all of her relationships, Taylor behaves with dignity and honesty. Particularly striking is her feeling for Estevan, the Guatemalan refugee.

She is physically attracted to him and believes, rightly, that he returns that attraction, despite his loyalty to his wife Esperanza. In several scenes Estevan and Taylor draw close to each other and almost reveal in words or action their love for each other, but Taylor realizes she cannot act on her feelings. She is deeply pained but quite clear that Estevan is unavailable to her.

Finally, Taylor's ancestral connection to the Cherokee people is important. Her great grandfather (13; this ancestor becomes a grandmother in *Pigs in Heaven*) had been one of the few Cherokees left in the Southeast when the tribe was marched, on the nineteenth-century Trail of Tears, from their forested and mountainous land to the barren and inhospitable land in Oklahoma which was given to them. Many of them died on the way, and they all suffered greatly. This transplanting, by force, of an eastern tribe to Oklahoma, was a particularly brutal event in the process through which the U.S. government acquired lands for settlers of European ancestry to occupy, a process which extended through most of U.S. early history and well into the nineteenth century. Its results are still being felt, as Kingsolver demonstrates. Mama and Taylor were aware that because of their partial Cherokee descent, they could qualify for "head rights" and become enrolled members of the tribe, if they were to choose to do so. They have never really seriously considered doing this, and neither of them has much knowledge of Cherokee culture or history beyond the most basic facts. But they always considered that they had an "ace in the hole" in their connection to the tribe. This connection becomes more significant in *Pigs in Heaven* than it seems in *The Bean Trees*, but even here it helps to relate Taylor to her adventures in acquiring a Cherokee foster daughter and falling in love with a Mayan refugee. She feels akin to each of them in a way that she might not have, had she not been aware of her own Native American heritage.

Turtle, who becomes her oddly named foster daughter, is given to Taylor by a desperate Native American woman in Oklahoma, who tells Taylor only three facts: the baby is the child of the woman's dead sister, the baby was born in a car, and she (the baby's aunt) cannot care for the child (18). The baby, nameless as far as Taylor knows, is wrapped in a blanket and strangely quiet. Unwrapping the child, Taylor discovers two things—that the baby is a girl and that she has been physically abused (22). Bruises on the child's body horrify Taylor and inspire her pity. The discovery of the abuse begins the process of Taylor's being drawn to the child and becoming determined to see that she never suffers abuse again.

The acquisition of the child occurs on the road, several states to the west of Illinois, where Taylor had adopted her own new name. The child also needs a name, and she acquires one based on her habitual clinging with tight little fists to Taylor. Taylor is reminded by this behavior of the mud turtles in Kentucky which refuse to let go after biting (22). The name comes to Taylor in almost the same moment as the discovery of bruises on the child's small body. Just as for Taylor, so too for Turtle, the acquisition of a new name is symbolic of the beginning of a new life. For Turtle, the choice is made by another, and it is only much later that it is revealed that Turtle had actually had another name. Her unexpected response to the name of the fourth month of the year leads Taylor and Lou Ann to believe that the child had originally been called April (128), and her official name becomes April Turtle Greer. But "Turtle," which as Taylor points out is an appropriate name for a child of Native American background, seems more suited to her and remains the name by which she is known. The discovery of Turtle's original name comes after her recovery is well under way, and the retention of Turtle as her name of daily use is seen as symbolic of her new life with her new mother. Ironically, "April" is an English name although it was given her by her Indian birth family, while "Turtle," which seems more typical of Indian naming customs, is given her by her white foster mother who takes her away from the Indian reservation of her heritage.

Turtle is a strangely silent child, who only slowly begins to talk. Her docility is unnatural. All this can be connected to the abuse she has suffered. At first she often seems oddly disconnected from the world, and this sinking emotionally into herself appears to be her method of coping with the physical abuse inflicted upon her. She gradually comes out of this withdrawal, but when she is unhappy or when a crisis occurs, she often reverts for a time to mental disconnection. In Taylor's casual but loving care, she begins to talk, but even her language is unusual. For some time her vocabulary is limited largely to the names of vegetables. In fact, she seems to see the world principally as a place where plants grow and bear fruit. When she does begin to talk, Taylor is so relieved that she is not very concerned about the child's strange vocabulary.

In fact, what Taylor had thought to be a late beginning to talking is much later even than she could have imagined. She has no idea of Turtle's age and, from her size and apparent development, had taken her for much younger that she actually is. A visit to a physician, some five months after Turtle is literally dropped into Taylor's lap, is eye-opening. Though Turtle is healthy and talking by this time, Taylor thinks that a doctor ought to see her because of the abuse evidences Taylor had observed. At first the doctor takes Turtle to be a healthy toddler of approximately two years old, but an examination reveals old, now healed, breaks in bones and indicates that she is more likely about three years old. He explains her delayed development as a "failure to thrive," caused by lack of love and care (121–23). The physical and sexual abuse Turtle had suffered, along with a generally unloving and neglectful environment, had led to her physical inability to grow and develop as well as to her delayed development and acquisition of other skills. All of this, gradually learned by Taylor, an inexperienced and unexpected mother, makes the child's growth and development into a generally happy and outgoing youngster even more startling.

The revelation of Turtle's original name, caused by her response to the word, is matched by another indication of a memory of her life before she came to Taylor. She often buries unexpected objects, apparently expecting them to grow, and Taylor connects this behavior with her concentration on vegetables and plant growth. As a part of Turtle's gradual growth into normal childhood, she first has a favorite flashlight she names "Mary" and plays with it like a doll. Later, she acquires a more appropriate toy, a real doll which she names "Shirley Poppy" and which she sometimes buries. Taylor realizes that this is related to Turtle's vegetable interests and that she believes that things, including dolls, which are buried in the ground will grow, blossom, and bear fruit. Late in the novel when they are on the road for a second time, Turtle unexpectedly reacts to cemeteries they pass. When Taylor is finally able to connect Turtle's reactions to cemeteries with her burying of Shirley Poppy and her references to "Mama," she realizes that Turtle had seen her mother buried (210). The loss of her birth mother presumably preceded her period of being physically abused. Taylor, now knowing something more of the pain that had filled Turtle's young life, is able to talk with her about death and loss and to try to reassure her that their relationship is firm and will endure, that while there are no guarantees, Taylor intends never to leave her. This memory, recovered by Turtle—or perhaps only discovered by Taylor—comes within a few pages of the end of the novel, just as Taylor is officially adopting Turtle. It thus becomes one more indication of Turtle's growth into a normal child with a happy home life and a future free from unnecessary pain and suffering.

Lou Ann becomes Taylor's closest friend and confidante in Tucson when Taylor begins to share her house. Lou Ann, like Taylor, has a baby in her care, but the two mother-child pairs differ in many important respects. Unlike Taylor, Lou Ann is married and the baby is her natural child, but her marriage is a troubled one. Angel, her husband, is irresponsible and keeps leaving her and Dwayne Ray, their baby. Ethnically, Angel and Lou Ann are different. Lou Ann, like Taylor, is a Kentucky native of Protestant heritage, while Angel is Hispanic and Catholic. Ironically, Lou Ann gets along better with her in-laws than with Angel himself. She is very passive, a more conventionally feminine woman than Taylor, and her pain over the breakup of her marriage seems to be almost as much a result of her fear of being without a man in her house as it is of her loss of her husband's love.

Like Taylor, Lou Ann changes during the course of the novel. She becomes more independent, and by the end of the book she is unafraid of being without a man. Her friendship with Taylor and Taylor's example of confidence and courage have helped her grow and mature. The two young women form a deep friendship, essentially a surrogate sister relationship. They help each other, confide in each other, care for each other's children, learn mothering skills from each other, and become wiser as a result of their relationship with each other. Though Lou Ann has been in Tucson for some time and can help Taylor learn about the city, it is Taylor who is more courageous about this life which is new to these transplanted Kentuckians and who is able to help Lou Ann become at home there.

If Lou Ann and Taylor become surrogate sisters, then their surrogate mother is Mattie, a less important character as far as the movement of the plot is concerned but a very important character for establishing several relationships and themes. She is an older woman who runs an auto repair shop in which Taylor finds a job. She is only one of several women with whom Taylor quickly builds warm, even loving connections and who assist Taylor because of their immediate response to her spunk and warmth. Equally important for Mattie's function in the novel is the fact that, above her auto shop, she runs a sanctuary for Guatemalan refugees who are fleeing persecution in their own country and are illegal immigrants in the United States. Her political activism introduces Taylor to wider concerns than Taylor had been aware of, and it also introduces her to Estevan and Esperanza, a Guatemalan refugee couple who will be instrumental in Taylor's emotional development.

Mattie is a strong woman, with the courage of Taylor and the maternal instincts of Lou Ann. She is a widow, running her own business quite capably and even using it as a cover for the political activities which are deeply important to her. Those activities include bringing refugees to her facilities, giving them shelter, feeding and clothing them, and trying to help them recover from the emotional as well as the physical results of the horrors they have undergone in Central America. Finally, she helps to move them on to other and safer locations, farther from the border with Mexico, where there are fewer immigration officials and where they are less likely to be detected and forcibly returned to their own country. That forced return would probably result in their imprisonment, torture, and execution, so Mattie's illegal activities are life-saving for the refugees but carry immense risks—for herself as well as the immigrants. Mattie is brave and strong, guided by intensely held convictions, she is a fine role model for her younger women friends.

The remaining characters of importance, both thematically and for the plot, are Estevan and Esperanza, a Guatemalan refugee couple. He is notable for his strength and integrity, and she is striking for her vulnerability and silent courage. Until the end of the novel, her name, which means "hope" in Spanish, seems deeply ironic for she is the only character completely lacking in hope. Both bear deep wounds as a result of their experiences in the brutal civil war being fought in their homeland. Their greatest loss, however, is that of their small child, stolen from them and presumably adopted, as many children were, by members of the majority faction. Thus, they can at least believe that the child is safe and loved, even while they mourn her loss. Estevan, a teacher of English in his former life, is educated and cultivated, and his knowledge and sophistication help to draw Taylor to him. Esperanza, on the other hand, still suffering deeply from her grief, remains withdrawn and even suicidal. She comes less alive as a character than does her husband, at least until the scenes near the end of the novel when she regains some vitality from her interaction with Turtle. Appropriately, the child who has now come out of her own catatonic state because of her foster mother's love is the one who is able to pull Esperanza back from her own withdrawal into some joy of life. The two, child and woman, are parallel in some ways, particularly their previous suffering which had led them to draw back from involvement in life and trust in people. They are further parallel in that both are called back to life by learning to care for particular others—for Turtle, the important other is Taylor, and for Esperanza, the important one is Turtle.

Estevan is a more crucial character than Esperanza because of the relationship established between him and Taylor. From the beginning they are attracted to each other, but that attraction is expressed only indirectly. Taylor always knows that Estevan's loyalty must belong to Esperanza, partly because of their marriage and history together but also partly because Esperanza needs Estevan while Taylor can survive without him. Taylor's and Estevan's mutual attraction comes closest to being admitted and expressed near the end of the novel, when they are about to separate for good. Thus, their near admission of caring for each other is also their farewell, and it is probably the realization that they do not expect to see each other again that enables them to admit to themselves and almost to each other what they are feeling.

The courage of Estevan and Esperanza is clear throughout the novel. Their political activity in Guatemala, which has led to their becoming refugees—people who no longer can live in the country which they love and for which they have already sacrificed greatly—is evidence of their bravery and integrity. Their merit is reemphasized when, in the last important action of the novel, they risk their freedom by agreeing to pose as Turtle's birth parents and pretend to give her up so that Taylor may officially adopt her. The pretense of surrendering custody of Turtle seems symbolically to Esperanza like losing her own daughter yet again, especially since on their drive from Arizona to Oklahoma Esperanza and Turtle have grown close and Turtle has succeeded in bringing Esperanza back into contact with the world. Had anyone suspected that the two Guatemalans were not Turtle's birth parents, the resulting investigation would surely have led to their being recognized as illegal aliens and returned to Guatemala, where they would have faced death. Thus, the risk they undertake out of friendship for Taylor and Turtle is great. Importantly, what they are trying to secure for Taylor—a safe parent-child relationship with Turtle—is exactly what they have lost with their own child. Their action, when its entire context is considered, is truly noble.

SETTINGS

The Bean Trees includes a number of important settings plus significant journey sections as Taylor moves from one place to another. Kentucky serves as an opening locale, the place from which she originates and which she leaves as soon as she can. Significantly, the novel's opening chapter is entitled, "The One to Get Away," referring to Taylor (then Marietta) as she escapes from the constraints of her early life in rural Kentucky. That setting is described as beautiful but lacking in opportunity. Young Marietta comes from a poor working-class family, reared by a single mother who does menial work in other people's homes in order to support herself and her daughter. The community is divided by class, and the Greer mother and daughter feel themselves imprisoned at the bottom of the class structure. Kentucky, then, represents the limitations of the East.

It is on the journey that Taylor acquires both her new name and her daughter. That journey seems rather oddly routed, though this is a minor point. Taylor drives westward out of Kentucky, yet her route takes her through a number of towns, mostly small, in central Illinois (Homer, Sadorus, Cerro Gordo, Decatur, and Blue Mound [12]), followed by Taylorville where she selects her new name. This route takes her well over a hundred miles north of any logical road westward out of Kentucky, and it seems chosen simply for the names of the settlements. From Illinois she drives westward as far as Wichita, Kansas, where, depressed by the Great Plains, she turns southward (12) into the Indian territory where she finds Turtle. From this point she heads westward, through Oklahoma and the Texas Panhandle and into Arizona until she reaches Tucson. Thus, the earliest and, in the long run, least thematically important portions of her journey seem almost random and unplanned. The Illinois miles are partly required by Taylor's need to acquire an appropriate name and partly by the author's delight in the names of several of the towns through which the character goes. Much of the rest of the trip is skipped over, with the portion from Oklahoma onward given the fullest description. It is this latter part of the journey which is retraced in reverse in the novel's final pages.

Arizona, particularly Tucson, becomes the opposite of Kentucky. It is where Taylor, renamed on her trip westward, ends up and where she establishes a new life free of the limitations of her hereditary class placement. Thus, Taylor retraces the westward movement of the pioneers who sought new opportunity in the West, where they believed they would be free from the restrictions of their pasts in the settled East. Taylor indeed does find a new life and new opportunities in Tucson. But she also finds poverty no less wrenching than that she had left behind. In settling into her new life in Arizona, Taylor is most at home with Lou Ann, largely because they are both transplanted Kentuckians who speak with similar accents, understand each other's pasts, and have essentially the same cultural backgrounds. The pull of childhood surroundings is strong, but Tucson and Arizona do become a new and hospitable world for Taylor. There she observes political courage in Mattie and her involvement in the sanctuary movement, and she learns about political corruption through Estevan and what he teaches her about the unrest in

Guatemala and the involvement of the United States in supporting an unjust regime there. Tucson is the beginning of a new life for Estevan and Esperanza no less than for Taylor and Turtle. Although Estevan, an English teacher in his native land, must work at menial labor as a dishwasher, he has the hope of a new freedom, and he and Esperanza have new friends, first Mattie and then Taylor, who are willing to take risks to ensure their safety.

In the middle, between the old and settled East of Kentucky and the new and more open West of Arizona is Oklahoma, where Taylor acquires Turtle, a child of the Cherokee Indian reservation. Taylor sees Oklahoma as bleak and foreboding. Observing the poverty and the grimness and sameness of life there, she is eager to go farther west. She had initially promised herself that she would drive westward as long as her car held out. But when it breaks down in Oklahoma, she finds that place so grim that she breaks this promise and continues westward. The barrenness of the Oklahoma that Taylor first sees is emphasized by the words of the woman who thrusts the child into Taylor's hands. She tells, not asks, Taylor to "Take this baby," and then identifies the child as being the offspring of her dead sister (17–18). When Taylor protests, the woman says, "This baby's got no papers," as if the child were a dog lacking American Kennel Club registration papers due to lack of pure breeding. She goes on, increasing the pathos, to say, "There isn't nobody knows it's alive, or cares. Nobody that matters, like the police or nothing like that. This baby was born in a Plymouth" (18). The land where a child can be so dehumanized and where no one cares is to Taylor brutal and ugly. When Taylor leaves Oklahoma, she sends a postcard to her mother saying that after all, she has "found my head rights. . . . They're coming with me" (23). She has at this point decided that her own Cherokee heritage is not the "ace in the hole" she and her mother had joked about. But ironically the Cherokee territory has given her something by which she is bemused, a child that she deeply pities but does not know what to do with. She and the child escape the land which seems so bleak to her and which has apparently meant neglect and serious physical abuse to the child. Arizona offers new life to both of them.

When Taylor and Turtle, now accompanied by Estevan and Esperanza, return to Oklahoma, with the dual purpose of delivering Estevan and Esperanza to a new and safer sanctuary and of making Turtle legally Taylor's daughter, Taylor learns that not all of Oklahoma is so bleak. She is told that there are mountains in Oklahoma and that the main portion of Cherokee lands lies in a much more beautiful area than she had seen. While she does not visit those lands, this information restores her faith in her and her mother's earlier fantasy and begins to suggest that Turtle's background and heritage may not be so completely sordid as Taylor had believed. (But the discovery of the actual Cherokee world must wait for a later novel, *Pigs in Heaven*.)

Two other locales, used briefly but symbolically in the novel, require mention. Two nature scenes are important for moving the plot forward and for deepening character development and relationships. The first occurs when Taylor, Turtle, and some of their new friends go on a picnic in the country. Taylor describes the setting as "a place you would never expect to find in the desert: a little hideaway by a stream that had run all the way down from the mountains into a canyon, where it jumped off a boulder and broke into deep, clear pools" (91). Estevan and Esperanza are new acquaintances, and Taylor's rapid and easy response to Estevan begins during this scene, though he is at this point a deep mystery to her. They all hike up the mountainside and eventually Estevan and Taylor swim in the cold water. This is just a brief moment out of their lives in the city, but it is deeply meaningful for Taylor.

Much later in Oklahoma, when Taylor is anticipating her parting from Estevan with whom she is by now deeply in love, she suggests that they prolong their time together by taking a brief side trip to Lake o' the Cherokees. Here they are clearly in Indian country, where Estevan, Esperanza, and Turtle all fit in, and where Taylor is the one who looks different. The land near the lake is rolling, green, and lovely, compared to the part of Oklahoma Taylor had seen earlier. She now realizes that the Cherokee lands and nation are worth knowing. At the lake they take a cottage, go rowing and swimming, and find refreshment in nature and each other. Estevan and Taylor almost wordlessly confess that they love each other but also acknowledge that this will be the last time they will see each other. Esperanza and Turtle grow close to each other, and Esperanza gains new hope and life as a result. Turtle's attempt to bury Shirley Poppy, resulting in Taylor's realization that Turtle had seen her birth mother buried, occurs here, so it is also in this scene that Taylor is able to reassure the little girl that she now has a mother who will not leave her. Though their relationship still lacks legality, it has deep emotional force. At the end of this brief chapter, Taylor suggests, and Estevan and Esperanza agree, that the Guatemalan couple pose as Turtle's natural parents so that Taylor may fraudulently but apparently legally adopt Turtle. Then Estevan and Esperanza will go on to their next sanctuary location, and Taylor and Turtle will return to Tucson. Thus, this scene is a time of recuperation and of healing as well as of parting. It balances the earlier nature scene which had been the beginning of the acquaintanceship of Taylor and Estevan. The contrast between the two scenes also reveals how far Turtle and Esperanza have come in their ability to love and to trust.

THEMATIC ISSUES AND CONCERNS

Kingsolver points out that many American authors do not like to be referred to as "political" writers, but she herself accepts that label with pleasure (see, for instance, *High Tide* 229–30). From the beginning, she has seen herself as an activist who is trying to change the world. Thus, her work is suffused with the ideas and principles she believes in. Antiwar sentiments, love of nature and concern for ecology, class concerns and support for working people, and feminist ideals are present throughout her work. Political fiction, it is often suggested by critics, naturally becomes propagandistic and preaches a particular idea or point of view instead of telling a story and creating character honestly and effectively. This is a danger of which Kingsolver is always acutely aware, and she strives to avoid preachiness by concentrating mainly on telling her story. In fact, one of Kingsolver's gifts is that of making ideas come to life by personifying them in complex and believable characters and placing those characters in believable, interesting plots. Her readers, however, if they are to achieve any full understanding of her work, must observe and consider thoughtfully the ideas presented in individual pieces of fiction.

The most obviously political theme in *The Bean Trees* relates to civil unrest in Guatemala. That the repressive and illegal government in that country is being supported by the United States, a very controversial issue in the United States for a period of years, is made plain by Estevan and Mattie as they teach Taylor about the impact of governments on ordinary people. The repression and cruelty of that Guatemalan government are indirectly shown in two ways. First, it is implied by the facts of Estevan and Esperanza's flight to Tucson, Mattie's involvement in helping them, and the very existence of the sanctuary movement. Secondly, it is directly described as Estevan tells Taylor something of the Guatemalan couple's experiences in their homeland, particularly the loss of their daughter, and we see the impact of this great loss in the brokenness of Esperanza. The Guatemalan issue was relatively current when

The Bean Trees was published in 1988, but now it seems only one of a series of conflicts in Central America in which the U.S. government has been embroiled over the years, generally on the side of right-wing governments or revolutions.

Present-day readers of *The Bean Trees* may not remember clearly or may not even know about the Central American conflict involved here, but that should not affect their response to the novel. Kingsolver gives her readers the information needed to comprehend her side of the controversy sufficiently so that they may understand the characters and their actions. That conflict can be seen simply as one example of U.S. involvement in Central America, the one which happens to be in progress when Taylor arrives in Tucson and, therefore, the one from which she learns about political oppression and activism. Thus, no special knowledge is required.

A part of Kingsolver's great gift as novelist is her ability to work information about specific historic political themes into the texture of her narrative. Two examples from *The Bean Trees* are particularly relevant here, one about the Guatemalan unrest and the other about child abuse. Margaret Randall has pointed out that an important theme in the novel is that of invasion. She defines this as having two aspects: "The sexual invasion of a child's body and the political invasion of a nation's sovereignty" (67). Thus, she ties together themes which are political on two different levels: Turtle's suffering and that of Guatemala, exemplified by Estevan and Esperanza. In each case, the theme is developed primarily through dramatization of the experiences of believable and likeable characters. But also in each case Kingsolver adds some specific information that may be useful to the reader who is not familiar with the background, historical or sociological, of the particular problem.

The political theme of Guatemalan oppression and the resulting flight of political refugees is dramatized by the presence of Estevan and Esperanza in Tucson, protected as they are by Mattie and the sanctuary movement. At first, hints are dropped of odd things occurring at Mattie's auto repair shop; then more specific information is relayed through a television news program in which Mattie is interviewed. A bemused Taylor watches it and is puzzled by some of Mattie's explanations of U.N. agreements. Equally puzzling to her is the statement by a representative of the Immigration and Naturalization Service, expressing doubts about Mattie's claims that refugees returned by force to their homelands are sometimes imprisoned or killed (103–4). The reader, who pieces things together from these clues, is given a context in which to place the actions and experiences of the characters in the novel. Taylor, however, lacking formal education, does not understand much of this, for she is not prepared to comprehend international laws or the general actions of nations. The information is nonetheless useful to her as she begins to try to understand her new friends.

Taylor does come to have a clearer understanding. The story of Estevan and Esperanza is gradually revealed to her, and her ready sympathies enable her to comprehend the suffering from causes so far different from her own experiences. She—and readers—achieve this understanding as Estevan bit by bit tells Taylor of his previous life. Particularly wrenching is the scene in which Estevan relates to Taylor the story of the loss of his daughter, Ismene. In order to explain how this could happen, he must also tell Taylor about the use of torture in Guatemala, about his and Esperanza's political activities, and about the killing of some of their friends and the capture of others, including Ismene. He had been forced to choose between trying to rescue Ismene and saving the lives of his friends. Having chosen the lives of his friends, he is comforted by the belief that Ismene is alive and growing up somewhere (134–39). Taylor perceives the great irony here, that Ismene's new family will doubtlessly rear her to hate insurgents like Estevan and Esperanza, thus tearing her from them symbolically a second time. Kingsolver skillfully uses this scene, with Estevan's explanations, to accomplish several purposes, giving information to the reader and helping Taylor understand Estevan, deepening their relationship.

The other political theme which is developed by both dramatization and explanation is child abuse. Turtle is the embodiment of this theme, and Taylor realizes that she is an abused child from the moment she opens the baby's blanket and discovers two important facts—her sex and the bruises on her little body. Turtle's withdrawal and slowness in learning to speak, in addition to her clinging to Taylor with her little clenched fists, illustrate some of the effects of the abuse she has suffered. Taylor takes Turtle to a doctor who describes the fractured bones and other physical evidences he sees of the treatment she had received. He also explains to Taylor the "failure to thrive" which has delayed her growth and development, making her seem about a year younger than her actual age. Later, after an incident in a park when Turtle is almost molested by a stranger and, as a result, reverts to something like her earlier, almost catatonic state, Taylor consults with a social worker, who relays some very specific information about child abuse, its effects, and state law regarding abused and neglected children (173–74). This information, useful to readers in creating a context for the action of the novel, also moves the plot forward, for it is as a result of this interview that Taylor realizes that she has no legal claim on Turtle and that if she wishes to keep the child whom she now deeply loves, she must somehow make their relationship legal. Thus, this scene leads directly into the final journey, with Estevan and Esperanza, back to Oklahoma and the mainly happy conclusion of the action of the novel. Once again, political theme, character, and action are powerfully intertwined.

Class is a less important theme but one which underlies much of the novel. Of the novel's characters, only Estevan, ironically the Hispanic illegal immigrant who stereotypically would be expected to be ignorant, is highly educated. Mattie, the widowed owner of an auto body shop and political activist, is the other important character not clearly a member of the working class. All the others are poorly educated, mostly working hard to scratch out a living. Taylor's mother had supported the two of them during Taylor's childhood by cleaning other people's houses and doing other menial work. Taylor works as a maid in a motel in Oklahoma in order to get enough money to repair her rattletrap of a car and proceed westward on her first journey. When she reaches Tucson, she is first employed in a fast food restaurant and then gets a job working for Mattie balancing tires and doing other physical work. Lou Ann gets a job working in a salsa factory, which Taylor describes as a sweat shop (151), but it is a job which Lou Ann loves. Taylor has a clear vision of class differences from the beginning, and she explains it to Estevan by describing her Kentucky high school in which all pupils fell into one of several clearly defined groups. Those who were town kids and middle class were at the top of the social hierarchy. Another group consisted of hoodlums. Finally, there were the "Greasers" and the "Nutters." A universally understood although unwritten rule was that there was "absolutely no mixing" (133) between the groups. Estevan quickly grasps her point and generalizes by comparing her Kentucky groupings to the Hindu caste system. Although the novel is not really about class, it sharply illustrates class through the characters and their situations. It demonstrates that though Taylor and her friends are uneducated and lacking in sophistication, they are kindly, loving, and full of life. Their kinship to the Nutters of Taylor's youthful memories does not mean that they are unworthy, as the town pupils then thought. Their rich humanity is stressed.

Another very important theme, directly related to Kingsolver's initial question about the ways in which people help themselves and others survive, is that of family, friendship, and community. In explaining to Estevan about the Nutters, Taylor had stressed that at least they had each other, that each of the groups formed a kind of community. Throughout her adventures, Taylor repeatedly makes friends and forms or becomes part of communities. When her car breaks down in Oklahoma, she quickly makes friends with the proprietor of a motel and as a result gets both a place to stay and work to support herself. In Tucson, arriving friendless with only her clearly disturbed foster daughter accompanying her, she soon makes friends with Mattie and gets a job working with her and then, answering a newspaper ad, finds a home and a new best friend in Lou Ann. From those two new connections, cemented very quickly by her recognition of their qualities along with her warmth and ability to offer deep friendship, follows the creation of a new community which widens to include Estevan and Esperanza as well as several neighbors.

One of the ways in which this theme is approached is through Taylor's and Lou Ann's attempts to define what a family is. Taylor resists a middle-class notion of family, expressing concern that she and Lou Ann are falling into a routine of daily life that makes them "like some family on a TV commercial, with names like Myrtle and Fred" (85). Later (in a motif taken from Kingsolver's own memories of childhood and repeatedly referred to in her work), Taylor remembers a family of paper dolls, with mother, father, daughter, and son, which she had had as a child. She thinks that she, Turtle, Lou Ann, and Dwayne Ray might "in a different world" have been like those dolls (138). By this time, Taylor and Lou Ann have begun to become a family, not just good friends who happen to live together and share the experience of rearing small children. Finally, at the end of the novel, separated from Lou Ann and Mama in two opposite directions by great distances and newly separated from Estevan whom she loves, Taylor accepts that she and Lou Ann have become a family, and both young women look forward to their reunion. In good humor she comments that she loves Lou Ann. She has realized all that the two of them have been through together and their intimate knowledge of each other has made them into a family (231). Families are created by love and living together, not just by biological relationship. She assures Turtle that they are now legally mother and daughter and that no one can separate them, and Turtle's song in the car, "Home, home, home, home" (232) expresses the goal of the final journey on which they are setting out and the accomplishment they have achieved in Tucson.

Related to the theme of family is the theme of motherhood. *The Bean Trees* examines several mother-child relationships. Chief among them is the informal connection of Taylor and Turtle, which demonstrates that true motherhood is not dependent on a genetic relationship. Taylor's foster motherhood of Turtle contrasts with Lou Ann's birth motherhood of Dwayne Ray. Neither of these young women is experienced or knowledgeable about parenting, but each loves the child in her care and because of her love and attention, each is a nurturing and effective mother.

These two active mother-child relationships contrast with two other parental links which are inactive: one because it has been forcibly broken and the other simply because the daughter has achieved maturity. Esperanza and Ismene's mother-daughter connection is in the past, Ismene having been literally wrenched from Esperanza's arms. The grief which Esperanza feels practically disables her, leading her to even attempt suicide near the end of the novel. Fittingly, it is her new and brief time with little Turtle which somehow begins her healing process. On the other hand, the only relationship including an adult child, that between Taylor and her Mama, persists. Although they are separated in space, they are connected by love and the companionship and understanding they feel for each other. Mama has successfully reared Taylor so that she is now independent and no longer needs the daily care and nurturing Mama once gave her. But the bond endures. Motherhood, then, as demonstrated by these characters can be an incredibly deep and lasting tie, one which is based upon the love and nurture of the mother, not necessarily requiring a literal birth relationship.

Another theme of importance to *The Bean Trees* is that of language. People recognize each other by their speech just as they are separated by differing uses of language. Language is a sign of humanity. Lou Ann and Taylor feel kinship with each other immediately because they speak alike. Their common upbringing in the working class of rural Kentucky has given them the same language, so they have an instant understanding of each other which neither of them has with anyone else. Estevan's polished English is one of the things which most quickly strikes Taylor about him. His comprehensive use of her own language inspires her to begin reading the dictionary and improving her own speech. A minor point of interest is his revelation that although both Estevan and Esperanza are of Mayan heritage, they have different Mayan mother tongues, and so they speak Spanish with each other. The emotional pain suffered by both Turtle and Esperanza is symbolized by their not-speaking, by their withdrawal from language. The damage done to Turtle is emphasized also by the fact that when she does begin to speak, her vocabularly is almost completely limited to words naming growing things—vegetables and other plants. Her interest in the fact that those plants grow from seeds is not explained until near the end of the novel, but her gradual transformation into a happy child is mirrored by her increasing use of a more varied vocabulary. Likewise, Esperanza's healing is paired with her slowly beginning to speak more, especially by her beginning to practice speaking English at the end of the novel. She needs to learn English for practical purposes, if she and her husband are to live in the United States, but the very fact that practical considerations have meaning for her is an indication of her return to something like normal life.

STYLE AND IMAGERY

Language, an important theme in this novel, is also central to its very essence. Taylor's rich, simple, and vivid Kentucky idiom gives the book its flavor and accounts for much of its appeal. Taylor's personality and her good humor are conveyed well by her direct, sometimes simple, and surprisingly poetic language. The novel's opening sentence illustrates the directness and use of vivid detail which characterize the novel: "I have been afraid of putting air in a tire ever since I saw a tractor tire blow up and throw Newt Hardbine's father over the top of the Standard Oil sign" (1). This opening draws readers immediately into the narrative. The following paragraphs tell the story of how the events summarized in the first sentence happened. This little story within the story catches interest by presenting an unusual phobia—after all, how many people have ever thought of any reason to be afraid of the air pressure in tires? Furthermore, it is told by a young woman who is afraid of almost nothing else. The story itself is funny, but no more so than any of a number of other episodes to follow, and thus it is a suitable opening for the novel. It also ties into the following action, for ironically the job Taylor finds in Tucson is in an auto repair shop, where one of her important tasks requires her to pressurize tires, mount, and balance them. The concrete detail of the novel's opening is also typical of the style of the remainder of the book. The name of the son of the victim and the brand of service station are not necessary, for neither figures into the novel's action, but these details help give flavor to the narrative and vividness to the reader's picture of the locale in which the events occur.

The characters' speech is vivid throughout. Kingsolver captures the

Kentucky idiom of Taylor and Lou Ann, with its Southern expressions, as well as their sometimes uncertain grammar. Speech is used to characterize and to give flavor to the narrative. Owned and run by Mattie, the Jesus Is Lord Used Tire Company where Taylor finds permanent employment despite her fear of exploding tires is comically named. Even Taylor finds the name odd, but it is only one of a large number of details offered by Kingsolver which help to give texture to the world in which these characters move.

One of the notable features of Kingsolver's style in this novel, as in all her fiction, is her use of imagery, especially imagery of plants and, somewhat less significantly, of animals. Birds are referred to frequently; the inadvertent capture and then release of a frightened bird is only one of a number of examples of sensitivity to and love of nature and natural creatures portrayed in the book. The title, one of the more obvious uses of plant imagery, is drawn from Turtle's fixation on vegetables. From a window in Lou Ann's house, Turtle sees wisterias and refers to them as "beans." Her puzzled foster mother realizes that she is referring to the pods created when some of the flowers have gone to seed and concludes that the transformation is "another miracle" (144). Much later, Taylor, having learned more about the life cycle of the wisteria, decides that the beans are a fitting symbol for the way people bind themselves to each other. Wisteria vines actually grow best in poor soil, surviving because the rhizobia (microscopic life-forms) that live on their roots change nitrogen from the soil into food for the wisterias. She tells Turtle that this "invisible system for helping out the plant" is "just the same as with people," and she lists some people they know who are interdependent (227–28). Thus, the bean trees of the title become a symbol for the question with which Kingsolver began the novel, the question about the ways in which people help each other survive.

Another particularly interesting symbol is a night-blooming cereus, a flower which only rarely and unexpectedly blossoms for a single night. The night before Taylor's return trip to Oklahoma is to begin, she and her companions are invited on short notice by some friends to come over for a surprise. The surprise turns out to be the magical blossoming of a previously undistinguished plant. They are entranced by its beauty, and Lou Ann sees it as an omen of something good. Turtle mispronounces its name as "See us," and ironically it is the blind Edna Poppy, the neighbor who knows from the scent when the flower is ready to blossom, for others are apt to overlook the homely plant in the corner of the front porch (185–86). The blossom of the cereus seems by its loveliness to transform the world and people around it, and in predicting something good it foreshadows the knitting up of plot strands at the end of the novel.

GENRE-BASED READINGS OF *THE BEAN TREES*

The Bean Trees is a political novel, developing themes related to causes prominent in the 1970s and 1980s, particularly to unrest in Central America as it impinged on life in the Southwest United States. The novel is based partly on the arrival of political refugees from Guatemala who were fleeing from persecution in their own country and who entered the United States illegally. The existence of the sanctuary movement, which also illegally helped and hid those refugees, comes at the center of the plot of *The Bean Trees*. However, this political theme also relates to themes of learning and growth present throughout the book. These latter themes offer another approach to interpretation of the novel. *The Bean Trees* may be seen as a variation of several genres, and examination of the novel in relationship to two of those genres enriches a reader's understanding of the complexity of Kingsolver's achievement in this book. Among these genres are two with impressive titles but rather simple definitions: the picaresque novel and the *Bildungsroman*, two types which are related to each other because of their reliance on similar basic characteristics.

The picaresque novel has a long history and includes such novels as Henry Fielding's *Tom Jones* and Mark Twain's *The Adventures of Huckleberry Finn*. It follows the travels and adventures of a male protagonist who is usually a rogue (or *picaro*). As a variation of this genre, *The Bean Trees* changes the male protagonist into a female and centers around an admirable main character, although Taylor's sense of mischief and willingness sometimes to cut corners are similar to characteristics of the more typical rogue. Picaresque novels are generally satiric, in that they examine and reveal the ills of society as the *picaro* experiences them, qualities also relevant to *The Bean Trees*. Further, the reliance on journeys to structure the book relates *The Bean Trees* to the picaresque, although the travels do not cover the entire novel, since much of its long middle is set in Tucson and indeed centers around the creation of home and community rather than around the motif of journeying.

More useful in analyzing Kingsolver's first novel is the concept of the *Bildungsroman*. Historically important and always popular, this type of

novel is often known by its German name, although it is also referred
to by English descriptors such as a "maturation," "education," or "coming of age" novel. Such a book generally centers around a young person,
naive and inexperienced at the beginning, who has a variety of experiences throughout his or her story and who learns from these experiences,
sometimes becoming wiser and more capable of living productively as
a result. Sometimes, however, the lessons are so bitter that the protagonist does not profit from them, becoming victimized by them instead.
It has often been argued, especially by recent feminist critics, that *Bil-
dungsromane* with female protagonists tend to show failures in maturation; that our culture and its expectations of women are such that girls
are not allowed to come to true maturity. These critics suggest that there
is an essential conflict between ideas of what is truly mature (independence, confidence, the ability to act on one's own principles) and what
is feminine (dependency upon a man, the desire to support and nurture
others). Thus, it is argued, the female protagonist must choose between
being mature and being feminine. Being feminine is generally accepted
as the goal for women in our society and is so inculcated in young female
readers that a "happy ending" requires that the female protagonist accept the stereotypically feminine characteristics and be rewarded by establishing a relationship with a man to whom she will be subordinate
and on whom she will depend. Such an ending requires that the female
protagonist *not* be independent and strong—exactly the opposite of the
qualities male protagonists of a typical maturation novel *must* develop.
Thus, the *Bildungsroman* is said to typically depict a failure in maturation as it shows a woman or girl becoming adjusted to her feminine
roles.

However, *The Bean Trees* shows several successful female maturations,
and of the important male characters, Dwayne Ray is an infant—too
young for significant maturation—and Estevan is essentially a static
character who is revealed but not allowed to develop and change. Most
obvious, although not the sort of maturation usually referred to in discussions of this genre, is Turtle's change from an almost catatonic,
harshly abused infant into a normal child who is able to respond naturally and happily to the world around her, secure in the care of people
who love her. Most significant are the lessons Taylor learns and her
maturation. Among other things, her lessons concern political activism,
love and loss, and motherhood. From the beginning she is an independent and courageous young woman, but she learns much about the pain
that goes with freedom, and she finds in herself the ability to behave

with dignity when her desires are counter to her knowledge of what is right. Deeply loving Estevan, for example, she never makes any attempt to win him away from Esperanza. Her maturation is at least partly dependent on her forming and participating in a set of relationships which strengthen and encourage her. Finding Mattie, her surrogate mother, and Lou Ann, her surrogate sister, as well as Turtle, her foster and then adopted daughter, enables her to establish a family that is broader than the birth family which consisted of only herself and her mother. She never rejects her relationship with her mother, but the new family, or community, she establishes in Tucson, supports her emotionally, and it is to that community she is ready to return in triumph after formalizing her adoption of Turtle at the end of the novel. It is notable that she is not rewarded by the love of a man. Both she and Lou Ann, the person now closest to her, accept their singleness (although Lou Ann, it must be admitted, appears to be entering a new relationship). Lou Ann, no longer grieving for the loss of Angel or fearful of being alone, and Taylor, having said goodbye to Estevan whom she loved but always knew she could not have, are now ready to go on together. Taylor expresses this in the final pages of the novel using the perspective of Turtle, as the two of them set out on their return from Oklahoma to Tucson.

> The sky went from dust-color to gray and then cool black sparked with stars, and [Turtle] was still wide awake. She watched the dark highway and entertained me with her vegetable-soup song, except that now there were people mixed in with the beans and potatoes: Dwayne Ray, Mattie, Esperanza, Lou Ann and all the rest.
> And me. I was the main ingredient. (232)

4

Animal Dreams
(1990)

Animal Dreams is Kingsolver's second novel and the first one she wrote purposely after beginning to consider herself a professional writer of fiction. Thus, it is more planned than *The Bean Trees* had been, and its narrative method, characters, and plotting are more carefully thought out, not developing naturally through the process of writing as in the earlier novel. Like *The Bean Trees*, and also like the novels to follow, *Animal Dreams* is a political book because Kingsolver is a political person. Also in keeping with Kingsolver's style, it began with a particular question of interest to the author. The question for *Animal Dreams* relates to Kingsolver's observations about differences among people, even among people molded by similar or identical environments. She wondered why individuals, even members of the same family, approach life very differently, some becoming involved and others detached (Fleischner 29). She invents two sisters through which to examine this conundrum. Quite naturally, because of her location in the Southwest and her interest in Central American politics and North American involvement in the internal affairs of these countries, she sets her story in Arizona and sends one of her characters off to Central America to participate in social action there. Surprisingly, however, she takes for her protagonist the detached sister, the one who avoids political and emotional involvement and never directly presents the sister who is more like Kingsolver herself. In this regard, *Animal Dreams* may be seen as an experiment to broaden her skills as a writer of fiction.

As Lisa See points out, this novel includes "all of her previous themes—Native Americans, U.S. involvement in Nicaragua, environmental issues, parental relationships, women's taking charge of their own lives" (47). Kingsolver herself acknowledged that this book "is about five novels," and for this reason she had difficulties pulling everything together. She used the image of skydiving to illustrate these problems: "About two-thirds of the way through," she told See, "I realized I wasn't *just* a fool; I had jumped out of a plane and the parachute wouldn't open" (47). But the book jacket had already been designed by her publisher, so she couldn't quit. Instead, she refocused on her initial question and was able to complete this very complex yet unified novel.

PLOT DEVELOPMENT AND SOURCE

The plot of *Animal Dreams* is a relatively simple one. A young woman, Codi Noline, returns to the town where she had grown up in order to teach in the high school for a year and to care for her father, who is in the early stages of Alzheimer's disease. He has been the town doctor, and the disease, which is beginning to rob him of his memory, will eventually kill him. As Codi goes to Grace, Arizona, her younger sister Hallie goes off to Central America to teach new methods of crop management to Nicaraguans who are embroiled in a nasty civil war. Hallie, who had always considered herself the lucky one, is kidnapped and then killed in Nicaragua. In Grace, where Codi had always felt herself an outsider, she discovers old friends, finds a new (and old) lover, participates in a struggle to keep the town from being destroyed, and rediscovers—and even discovers—her real roots.

The action of the novel comprises essentially the academic year which Codi spends in Grace, although a brief epilogue occurring several years later gives the book its final emotional conclusion. It is mostly told straightforwardly, although it is rich with details of the daily lives of Codi and the others who live in Grace and with complex characterizations which introduce Mexican-American and Native American customs and beliefs. The plot relies heavily on internal, emotional action and on the vivid depiction of a multicultural, remote community.

Kingsolver always maintains that she does not write directly from life. Thus, her characters are not herself and their stories are not hers. She does, however, employ her own experiences at times in all her novels. In *Animal Dreams* she makes important use of lessons she had learned in writing her journalistic account of the 1983 strike against the Phelps Dodge Mining company in several southern Arizona towns. *Holding the Line: Women in the Great Arizona Mine Strike of 1983* concentrates, as its subtitle indicates, on the experiences of women during what was a sometimes violent struggle. The women of the company towns whom Kingsolver interviewed found new courage and resolve during that strike, and they served as models for some of the characters in *Animal Dreams* who have similiar experiences. Like the actual towns of the strike, the fictitious Grace of *Animal Dreams* has had its waters poisoned by pollution from mines and its crops ruined as a result. Kingsolver transforms the events of the strike for her own purposes, and the novel contains no labor unrest. It does, however, demonstrate how simple people can stand up against a powerful company and how they can find in the skills of their daily lives the tools to fight against injustice.

STRUCTURE AND NARRATIVE METHOD

In *Animal Dreams*, structure, or organization, and narrative method, or the way in which the story is told, are intimately connected with each other. The novel alternates between sections told by Codi, the protagonist, or central character, and sections told in third-person narration using the point of view of Doc Homer, her father. Each section is titled with the name of the respective narrator, either "Cosima" or "Homero." That Cosima is Codi's actual name is revealed early in the narrative, but Codi always refers to her father as "Doc Homer," and his actual name is given as Dr. Homer Noline. That he was by birth Homero Nolina and that the title of his sections is his real given name is not revealed until Codi learns this information late in the novel. Codi's sections, in which most of the novel is told, predominate, several of them containing as many as five chapters. Homer's sections, on the other hand, are quite short, only a page or two in length.

Differences in grammatical tense are significant. Codi's sections are told, as is most common, in the past tense and generally consist of rather straightforward narrative, although they are often complicated somewhat by containing memories, depicted through flashbacks which reveal what she is presently thinking and feeling as well as what she is presently troubled about. Homer's sections, on the other hand, flow back and forth between past and present tenses, although past tense often predominates. These differences in tense are symbolic of the two characters' awareness of time. Codi, a somewhat too rational person who sees the world basically from a scientific viewpoint and finds little meaning in most of her life, uses the conventional past tense. For her, time is simply something that flows past and there is little significance to the relationship between past and present events except as past experiences cause her pain.

Doc Homer, on the other hand, in the early stages of Alzheimer's disease, is losing his awareness of the differences between past and present. For him the past often is the present, or at least it is more real than his current actuality. Thus, the novel opens in the present tense, describing Homer looking down at his sleeping daughters and yearning over them. Typical for him, he loves them but cannot express that love and can only fear what is to come for them. This moment occurred years earlier, long before the action proper of the novel begins, but to Homer, it is as real as his present life. For him, experiences of past and present flow together, and in some of his brief sections, he moves back and forth between memory of the past and action in the present without distinguishing between them. He seems intuitively, in the throes of his terrible illness, to understand how the past has affected his family, especially his emotionally crippled older daughter Codi. She, on the other hand, perfectly sane and rational, lacks the ability to connect and understand all her experiences. She knows she has been terribly wounded by her past, but she cannot remember much of her childhood, and aside from the stillbirth of her child she seems out of touch with much that has formed her. The uses of tenses in the narrative sections associated with "Cosima" and with "Homero" underline these truths, although they will not be completely clear until the end of the novel.

The use of sections tied to two major characters is *Animal Dreams*'s most obvious structural device. More subtle is the book's framing by the motif of the Roman Catholic liturgical celebration of All Souls, a motif also developed importantly within the narrative. The brief chapter which is the opening section of the novel showing Doc Homer watching his two daughters sleep bears the title "The Night of All Souls." Dr. Homer Noline, here referred to by his full name, silently watches his daughters, also called by their full given names, Cosima and Halimeda, as they sleep, "curled together like animals whose habit is to sleep underground, in the smallest space possible" (3), in the novel's opening sentence. The date is specifically identified by the chapter's title as All Souls' night, and actual placement in chronological time will soon be clarified as occurring years before the novel's main action. Only later, when Doc Homer's mental affliction and his confusion of past and present become clear, will the actual timing of this brief episode emerge. The chapter concludes by emphasizing his love for his daughters and his separation from them, his grieving over "the river he can't cross to reach his children" (4). It also suggests their interdependence on each other.

A crucial chapter, a bit less than midway through the novel, picks up the motif of All Souls and bears a title which uses the name given by Mexicans to All Souls' Day, "Day of the Dead." Since All Souls' Day comes at the beginning of November, the events in this chapter occur early in the action of the book, which is centered around one academic year at the high school in Grace. In quick succession, Codi learns that a pregnant pupil is about to drop out of school, teaches an impromptu lesson on birth control, and worries about the pollution of the river which has caused the death of the microscopic life-forms which nourished it, as well as about the approaching destruction of the town by a dam built by the mining company which has polluted the river. She also visits her ailing father, receives a treasured letter from Hallie, and then observes the children trick-or-treating on Halloween. The celebration of Halloween is an indication of the Americanization of Grace, but it is followed by observances related to the villager's Mexican and Spanish heritage. Codi comments that some of the people attended Mass on the Roman Catholic holiday of All Saints on November 1, but that everyone observed All Souls on the following day, November 2, by going to local graveyards to tend and decorate family graves, including graves of otherwise forgotten ancestors. Codi goes to the graveyard with her friend Emelina Domingos and Emelina's children and mother-in-law, although she feels like an outsider since, as she had always been told, her family came from Illinois. It is at this time that she makes a momentous discovery, finding the graves of a family called "Nolina," only one letter different from her own last name of "Noline," and she jokes about the Nolinas being her relatives until she notices the grave of a man called "Homero Nolina." She asks about the Nolinas and learns only that they were considered trash despite being descended from one of the founding Gracela sisters and that they are now "about gone" (164) from Grace. Codi begins to guess that these Nolinas are connected to her own family, and this discovery is crucial to her final discovery of herself. From the dead identified here will eventually come the re-creation of her identity and her finding new life at the end of the novel.

Having begun with "The Night of All Souls" and having made special use of the motif of All Souls, or the holiday of the Day of the Dead, *Animal Dreams* returns to this motif in the novel's final two sections, both brief. One of these sections is given to Doc Homer, whose identification as "Homero" is now clear; the final one belongs to Codi and serves as a kind of epilogue, occurring several years after the rest of the action of the novel. Doc Homer's section, called "Human Remains," consists of a conversation between Codi and her father in which they finally are able to be honest—and even openly loving—with each other. Thus, it ties up many of the emotional strands of the novel. Finally, in Codi's section, the novel comes to a fitting close, entitled "Day of All Souls." This section is specifically dated as the year 1989, the only exact year given in the novel. Codi once again goes with her friends to the cemetery to decorate graves, but now she has the grave of her father, dead two years, and the graves of all the other Nolinas to care for. Then she goes to the place where she had, as a small child, seen her mother die. It is fitting that she has chosen the day on which the souls of all the dead are memorialized finally to remember both her mother and father. Having recaptured her memories and love for them, she now can care for them and their forebears. She is freed by these very actions to look to the future instead of to the past. She is pregnant, and this baby, contrasting with the youthful miscarriage which has long tortured her, will be full term, healthy, loved by both of its parents. The novel comes full circle here in terms of its structure, but its emotional ending, for Codi, is very distant from where it began.

SETTINGS

Broadly, *Animal Dreams* is set in Arizona, but aside from a few references to Tucson and the evocation of Central America in Hallie's letters, the two most important locales are the small and remote town of Grace and, briefly, the much more remote Santa Rosalia Pueblo. Most of the action takes place in Grace; its history as a town, its people, an unusual aspect of its animal life, and its current precarious position are sharply delineated. When Codi first returns to Grace after an absence of many years, she finds familiar sights: the Hollywood Dress Shop, with its "ferocious display of polyester" (11), Jonny's Breakfast, the State Line Bar, and the Baptist Grocery call up images of dusty rural small towns everywhere. Even though Codi is returning to her childhood home and expects to live in the guesthouse of an old high school friend, she is immediately overcome by her old feeling of being an outsider. Believing that her forebears were from Illinois and that her heritage was Anglo, she feels no connection with this small and ingrown, mainly Mexican-American community. To her, "Grace looked like a language I didn't speak" (12).

Orchards, a mining company, and the railroad have been the mainstays of Grace's economy. The railroad takes the men it employs away from the community, and the mining company has so polluted the waters that the orchards are now dying. The community's one doctor is suffering from Alzheimer's disease and can no longer care adequately for his patients. Yet, the community, which centers on its women, retains a vital folk life. The high school in which Codi teaches seems little different from schools elsewhere—girls get pregnant, and many pupils are rebellious, marking time until they can leave. Still, Codi's pupils respond to her unorthodox teaching methods and learn from her to care about the effect the mining company's irresponsible activities has on their world. Here, Kingsolver is clearly drawing on the knowledge of small southern Arizona towns which she gained while writing *Holding the Line*.

Culturally the community is strongly Mexican. Such holidays as All Souls, are characteristic. The names of the people are Spanish, and there is some use of the Spanish language. Family relationships, as revealed in the family of Emelina Domingos, Codi's close friend, retain the closeness typical of their heritage, with the grandmother playing a very influential role in daily life.

But Grace is also distinctive, largely because of its special history. Over a century earlier, nine sisters surnamed Gracela and all with blue eyes had come from Spain to marry gold miners, bringing with them their pet peacocks. The peacocks had thrived and multiplied—their descendants now run wild in the canyon where Grace is located. Further, the descendants of the Gracela sisters bequeathed their blue eyes to their children, so that the dark-haired villagers often bear unexpectedly light eyes. That the gene pool of Grace is seriously inbred is revealed by an unusual genetic phenomenon which Doc Homer had studied: the briefly marble-eyed babies who began to be born in the 1950s as a result of the intermarriages of third cousins.

The presence of such inbreeding might stereotypically suggest a dying population handicapped in other ways, such as feeblemindedness. But this is not true of Grace. The town has a vibrant culture, primarily of Mexican origins. The people retain the custom of making piñatas, to be used at Christmas, and the employment of this skill, combined with the use of the always present and beautiful peacock tail feathers, enables them to raise a great deal of money very quickly and, thus, to mount an effective campaign against the mining company's plan to build a dam which will destroy their polluted home place. The women are central to the world of Grace. These women are seen in two ways: partly in the active home life, casual but effective parenting, and passionate wifehood of Emelina Domingos, Codi's old friend and landlady; and partly in the presence of the mostly older ladies of the Stitch and Bitch Club. These latter make up the force which, when angered by the mining company's actions, takes immediate action, first to raise money and then to carry on a publicity campaign about what Black Mountain Mining is doing to the town. There is little defeatism in Grace, primarily because of the dynamic and forceful women.

Although the village is largely Mexican-American in culture, it is also the center for a significant Native American population, with members of three tribes represented. Loyd Peregrina represents these ethnic strands, considering himself basically a Pueblo, although he also has Apache and Navaho in his background and speaks all three Native languages. He attended Grace High School, where he and Codi had their first relationship, and he was a leader there. But his home—and his emotional ties—are, significantly, with his Pueblo mother and family. The novel contains several important scenes set in Native American surroundings, two almost idyllic and one horrible. The horrible one is the scene in which Loyd demonstrates his great skill as a handler of fighting cocks as Codi watches. The cockfight occurs on the reservation, and this activity is one which Loyd had inherited from his father. The cruelty of the activity, however, is not presented as a particularly important part of Native American culture, although its barbarity is in no way underestimated, and this scene contrasts markedly with what immediately follows.

Two scenes take us to living sites, one ancient and one presently in use, of the Pueblo Indians. On the same outing as the cockfight, Loyd takes Codi to a ruin, which he calls Kinishba and defines as "prehistoric condos" (127). He leads her through the old walls, as she wonders at their size and complexity. When she is startled by the depth of the walls, he tells her that they are essentially graveyards—dead babies would be walled up in them to be kept close by their families (128). Kinishba is, he tells her, eight hundred years old. When she comments on how natural it looks, more as if it grew from the land than as if it had been built by people, he explains that the goal of the Pueblo builders had been to create something that did indeed look as if it had sprouted naturally from Mother Earth, something that "Mother Earth will want to hold in her arms" (129). The peace of this place and the magic it weaves around both Codi and Loyd make it appropriate that this is where they make love for the first time as adults in their new relationship with each other.

Later, in a scene that the visit to Kinishba had seemed to foretell, Loyd takes Codi to his mother's home, Santa Rosalia Pueblo. In a symbolic action, he changes from his cowboy boots into moccasins before entering so his mother will not say, as she often has, that he looks like a Navaho. Though Loyd in some ways is, as he calls himself, a mongrel, he respects his mother's Pueblo identity and reclaims it when he visits her. Codi notices that the village blends into its surroundings nearly perfectly, just as Kinishba had done. Unexpected things from outside mix with peculiarly Native sights—there is a basketball hoop on one house and in Loyd's mother's home there is an electric sewing machine and a radio plays country music, while a baby nestles on a cradle-board that is lined with fur (227–30). Their visit occurs at Christmas. But the language is Pueblo, and the food and the customs are Native American. The dance with which they celebrate is distinctive of the people. Particularly interesting is Loyd's explanation of the kachina Koshari who plays an important part in the dance. Loyd points out that the kachinas, which most Anglos know only as dolls, are also dancers and spirits and, it is implied, symbols, for he compares them with Santa Claus and refers to the crucifixes in homes in Grace as "Jesus kachinas" (238).

The spirituality of the Pueblo people and their closeness to what Loyd calls Mother Earth, along with the loving and close family relationships in this matriarchal family, are most characteristic of the depiction of Santa Rosalia Pueblo. Loyd is surrounded by female relatives, who love him deeply and give him a strong sense of rootedness that enables his clear sense of belonging, his very identity. The women are equally accepting of Codi, who finds in Loyd's home a very special and welcoming place, despite her initial feelings of being a complete outsider.

CHARACTER DEVELOPMENT

Although Kingsolver began with a question rather than with a character or an event, *Animal Dreams* is more dependent on character than her other novels. This follows naturally from the fact that her question related to differences among individuals and how those differences come about, even in members of the same family who would, presumably, have shared the same environment as well as the same heredity. The author has chosen to build her novel around the two very different sisters, Codi and Hallie: one a detached, sad, persistently pessimistic and insecure young woman, and the other an involved, happy, optimistic, and confident person. In some ways the differences between the sisters are similar to the contrasts between Taylor Greer and Lou Ann Ruiz in *The Bean Trees*. The novel follows Codi's experiences, and Hallie never appears directly, being revealed only in Codi's memories of her and in her letters to Codi. The remaining character of obvious importance to the book by providing one of the two points of view used is Homer, the physician who is the father of both young women. Intentionally isolated and unhappy, even embittered, he appears more like Codi than Hallie in character and response to the world and his experience of it. However, both Hallie and Homer are static, that is, more or less unchanging, throughout the course of the novel, while it is Codi who struggles to understand why each of them is as she or he is, as well as to learn about her own identity and family heritage. Because of her centrality, other characters can often be examined and understood primarily as they impinge upon or reveal Codi.

Cosima Noline, always called Codi, narrator of most of the novel, is presented as a young woman of great intelligence and important gifts who chooses not to make use of her abilities. Like Lou Ann of *The Bean Trees*, she is passive. She drifts aimlessly, without goals or hope that her life can have meaning. She lives with a man whom she does not love, and her relationship with her sister, to whom she always feels inferior, is the most important emotional commitment, perhaps the only true emotional connection, in her unhappy life. Although she has nearly qualified to become a physician, she throws away a potential career of service and healing, working instead at a series of jobs which do not challenge her and in which she finds no fulfillment. At various times she works in fast-food restaurants or as an artist's model. As the novel begins, she is returning to Grace, the village where she was born and raised, to serve for a year, on the basis of temporary teaching credentials, as a high school biology teacher. The fact that her qualifications for the job are marginal and temporary is symbolic of her attitude toward life. She sums herself up well as a "bag lady with education" (259).

The novel asks several questions about her: Who is she? Why has she become an emotional cripple? Why does she consider herself a failure?

Is there any possibility of her finding herself and becoming emotionally healthy and committed to something? Her story is a retreat from an unsatisfying life, a return to the home where she had never felt she belonged, and a reunion with the father she believes does not love her. All of this leads to a series of discoveries about herself, her background, and her possibilities. At the same time, she recaptures childhood memories which she had thought she lacked, a symbol of the wholeness she is achieving by the end of the novel.

In returning to Grace for the expressed purpose of looking after her aging father, now diagnosed by himself as suffering from the early stages of Alzheimer's disease, Codi is fleeing from her unsatisfactory life. She had been living in Tucson with her lover, Carlo, and her sister, Hallie, and was convinced in her usual way that Carlo cared more for Hallie than for herself. She herself loves Hallie deeply and is dependent on their mutual relationship much more than she cares for Carlo, whom she stays with more out of habit than any emotional connection. Hallie is going off to Central America and their father is not well; nothing much holds Codi to Tucson when she is told by an old friend that a teaching position for which she might qualify is open in the Grace high school. In her usual aimless way, not believing that she would ever get the position, Codi applies for it and is surprised to be hired. Thus, her life changes at the same time as Hallie, quite intentionally, makes a change in her own.

One of the opening scenes of the novel sets up Codi's sense of helplessness and leads naturally to the introduction of her many losses. Among her losses are the death of her mother, her childhood failure to rescue some coyote pups from a flood, the concealed miscarriage of her baby when in high school, and finally the new and devastating loss of her sister. All of these losses, particularly those from the past (not including the loss of Hallie), are related in making Codi feel helpless, unable to affect events, and thus, worthless. Sadly, almost as soon as Codi reaches Grace, memories of one of the early losses which have formed her impinge on her awareness.

She arrives in Grace, feeling herself a stranger, and immediately is reminded of one of the oddities of this remote town—the peacocks which are everywhere, having been brought from Spain long ago by the Gracela sisters. She hears their raucous calls and sees one of them in a tree being tormented by children who are poking at it with long sticks. The peacock's helplessness reminds her of her own powerlessness, and the fact that it has no defenders seems like her own lack of protection from her various losses. She tries to stop the children from what she sees as their cruelty, only to realize that the peacock is not a live bird but a piñata, a figurine made of clay and crepe paper and filled with candy meant to be broken by children. Thus, her attempt at rescuing the bird is not only futile but silly. This misadventure makes her feel like even more of an outsider for having so completely misunderstood a child's game in which she had herself participated some years earlier. But her reasons for trying to intervene are perfectly in keeping with her sense of herself and her world as well as with her previous experiences.

Her losses began early, with the death of her mother after Hallie's birth. She has a memory, which others tell her cannot be real, of a helicopter and her mother's dying before it could take her to treatment. Only late in the novel does one of the women of the village reveal to her that she had indeed been present at her mother's death and that her memory is complete and true. The woman had brought the child Codi to the scene believing that she had a right to be there with her dying mother despite her father's refusal to allow this. Codi learns that her memory had in this case been more accurate than what she had been told. She cannot regain her mother, but she can at least recapture her memory of her own presence at the moment which came close to destroying her family. She can connect that memory with the "sense" she had always had "of her [mother] that was strong and ferociously loving" (49). Learning the truth of this memory allows Codi to regain something of the family she lost so long ago at her mother's death and her father's resultant withdrawal. From this loss there is some healing.

Another loss, less explicitly tied into the course of the novel but mentioned several times, occurred when she and Hallie tried, at great risk to themselves, to save a litter of coyote pups from a flood. They were unable to rescue the animals, and as usual Codi blames herself. The motif of animal cruelty, presented first in the piñata scene and picked up in Loyd's involvement in cockfighting, has its earliest chronological occurrence in this episode. From this loss, no healing follows.

The loss which most affected the person Codi has become is that of her baby, a loss which, in addition to the loss of her mother, framed her earlier life in Grace (50). After a few dates with Loyd, a popular and attractive high school student, the then fifteen-year-old Codi became pregnant. Always thin, she managed to hide the pregnancy from everyone except her physician father, who was never able to reveal to her his knowledge and concern. Feeling completely alone, she bears the stillborn baby prematurely and buries it secretly. Her grief over the baby's death is deep, and harder to bear by the fact that she believes she has no one with whom to talk about it. She had never told Loyd about her pregnancy, and even when during the course of the novel they again become lovers, she holds her secret to herself, considering it only her business and having nothing to do with him.

Eventually, healing for this great loss begins. Codi tells her father of her pregnancy, only to learn that he has known of it all along, that he watched her bury the little body (260). Several plot threads are tied together in a single conversation, and Codi resolves several problems by talking them out, finally, with Doc Homer. He acknowledges his descent from the Nolinas of Grace, his awareness of her pregnancy and loss of the baby, and the hurt that has incapacitated him emotionally. Understanding that his losses were as deep as her own and that the two of them had sought to cope similarly, by withdrawing emotionally, she can now begin to find peace. As a result, she is able to ask her father to take her to the baby's grave, for one of her more significant memory lapses has been of its location (289).

Near the end of the novel, after she has lost Hallie and is being forced to acknowledge her experience and what it has done to her, she sums up her past. To a well-meaning stranger on the bus away from Grace, as she is fleeing from Loyd and her father as well as from her unexpected success as a teacher, she angrily says, "My mother died when I was little and my father will probably be dead before the year's out, and my baby died, and now my sister is dead too" (316). Both anger and grief motivate her at this moment. But after running away from Grace to return to Carlo whom she does not love and therefore with whom she can live without risking any more losses, she returns to Grace, where she tells Loyd about the baby and shows him the baby's grave (332), although neither visit to the grave is directly described. As a result of this most important healing, Codi finally learns to hope and is able to think about possibilities of building a future with Loyd. Her pregnancy in the novel's epilogue is a fitting conclusion to her story of loss.

The most important character to the conception of the novel, although not to its action, is Hallie because she represents a kind of ideal: the person who cares about life and others, one who is willing to take risks to live by her beliefs. Ironically, she is the one important character who is never seen directly. What is revealed is her influence on Codi and Codi's love for her and sense of inferiority to her younger sister. Hallie is the one who always had purpose, who always knew what she wanted to do and be, and who always succeeded at reaching her goals. A specialist in botany, she had run a hotline in Tucson, which people could call with questions about their plants, and she did this well, as Codi is reminded by running into people who remember Hallie's assistance to them. Hallie wants to make a difference in the world and cannot live a life which selfishly, in her view, does not help others.

The two sisters, separated by distance in both space and attitude, carry on an impassioned correspondence through letters. In one of these letters Hallie tries to explain how she lives her life. She maintains that it is much simpler than Codi had been trying to make it. She isn't trying to reform the world, she says. It is only that she couldn't "subsidize" the war by not joining it, that she had to choose sides (299). She goes on to state her conviction "that the very least you can do in your life is to figure out what you hope for. And the most you can do is live inside that hope" (299). She also enumerates some of the things that make up her hope: enough to eat, people being kind to each other, and the possibility for children to grow up happy, healthy, and productive. These are simple desires, she says, but they are important enough to her that she must dedicate a part of her life to them. At the same time, she tells Codi to stop feeling inferior to her and to decide what her own hopes are so that she can live in them. At the end of the novel Codi finally realizes that Hallie had simply wanted to save herself, "[j]ust like we all do" (334).

Although Hallie is equally as important as Codi for the development of Kingsolver's central theme she is much less significant in obvious ways. She never appears directly—her voice is revealed only in her letters—and she does not become nearly as rounded as does Codi, or as do a number of the other characters. This is a result of both her being kept offstage and the fact that she comes too near to being presented as an ideal to come truly alive as a real person. While we learn something of her frustrations, irritations, heartaches, and even angers in her letters, these are not enough to make her as believable and complete a character as her deeply flawed sister becomes.

She is, however, in Codi's consciousness a powerful force in the novel. Codi's love for her is deep and strong, and Codi thinks of her younger sister often, with love, admiration, and longing; she worries about Hallie a great deal. Thus, Hallie's presence, while indirect, is still crucial. After her death, Hallie becomes something of a heroine. Codi had carried on a publicity campaign in an attempt to free her sister from captivity, and although the resulting news coverage was often politically slanted in ways that would have horrified Hallie, Codi receives letters after her sister's death from people who admired Hallie and her work. Most important, however, are the private effects of Hallie's life on Codi. As girls they had been inseparable, although it would seem that Codi, as the elder, had been something of a leader. What finally becomes clear to Codi, as she tries to sort out their differing personalities, is that although they were sisters who experienced what are usually considered the formative years of life together, they had actually "grown up in different families" (283). Finding some of the drawings they had made as children, she observes a crucial difference. Her own show a complete family, with stick figures of a mother, a father, two little girls, and a house with the sun shining down on it. Hallie's, on the other hand, show only two little girls holding hands with each other (282–83). While Codi had known a complete nuclear family and then been deeply wounded by the death of her mother and the emotional withdrawal of her father, Hallie had not known either the intact family or the losses. To her, life with a loving sister to whom she was deeply bonded was normal. Although her world, her family, was defective by many definitions, it was stable, unlike Codi's.

Homer Noline, doctor for the village of Grace and father of Codi and Hallie, is in some respects an enigmatic figure. He is presented through his own sections in which his often confused point of view is dramatically rendered, and he is also seen through Codi's comments and attitudes about him. Since he is often uncertain as to when he is in time and since Codi has greatly conflicting notions about him, the complexity and ambiguity of his characterization are not surprising. His impact on Codi is presented as negative, automatically making him an unpleasant character, but Kingsolver lessens this negativity by giving him the first few pages of the novel. Here he is shown to be loving and in deep pain over his inability to keep his daughters from suffering. His suffering from the terribly debilitating and eventually fatal Alzheimer's disease also helps to create sympathy for him. Finally, his suffering over the death of his wife, which has caused his emotional withdrawal, clarifies his behavior. He, no less than Codi, has been affected by that loss.

His life is built on a deceit and a concealment. The deceit is about his true background and parentage, and seems to be only partial. He is actually twice a descendent of the Gracela family: his father born from a line now disreputable and considered trash by the people of Grace, and his mother coming from a prominent and respected line. His mother had married his father against her family's will. Because of his sense of shame at being a member of the ostracized Nolinas, ingrained in him from childhood, Homer joined the army, got his medical education through the G.I. Bill, and took his wife to Illinois. When they returned, he had changed his name to "Noline," a thin disguise, and she apparently had discarded her birth name "Althea," an important name in the Gracela family, and became "Alice." He claimed to be from Illinois, and in this belief he raised his two daughters. Eventually he acknowledges to Codi his deception, accepting that he had become "a man with no history" who "didn't redeem my family" but rather "buried it and then I built my grand house on top of the grave" when he changed his name (287).

He believes that the people have been fooled by his deception, but Codi tells him this is not true. He has deceived himself even about Grace's acceptance of him and his family. He has become a good doctor and is loved as such. That he has been a highly regarded physician is obvious. Recognizing that all is not right with him, the women of the village bring food to fill his refrigerator. They speak fondly of him and inquire about him frequently. They have entered into a silent conspiracy allowing him to believe his secret is truly his own, despite the fact that they know otherwise. They have forgiven him, although Codi suspects they retain their feelings of guilt over their own part in causing his shame about his family (288).

The concealment, which accompanies the deceit about his background, involves Homer's love for his daughters. After his wife's death, as Codi puts it, he "kind of took [his] phone off the hook, emotionally" (288). Throughout their childhood, the girls felt their father's presence only in the ugly orthopedic shoes he forced them to wear. Hallie did not especially miss his presence, for she had never known it, and her sense of family was constructed on herself and Codi. Codi, however, having known a complete family with two parents and a sister, deeply missed and needed the parental care which Doc Homer was no longer able to give. That he loved—and loved deeply—is demonstrated in the novel's opening chapter. That he was unable to show that love is dramatized in what his detachment has done to his elder daughter.

Two activities, one medical and one recreational, characterize his relationship with the world. Some years earlier, he had taken advantage of the fact that the population of Grace had become somewhat inbred because of its isolation, resulting in certain physical characteristics being particularly prominent. Doc Homer made a study of an oddity of pigmentation which produced babies who are "marble-eyed" (71) at birth, although their eyes soon appear normal, and published his findings in a genetics journal. Over the years, he photographed the babies who showed this trait. These photographs at first add to Codi's sense of alienation because she sees them as totally unrelated to herself. But eventually they become a clue to her family's actually belonging in Grace when she discovers pictures of herself and Hallie as babies with those same eyes (284). The genetic study reveals Doc Homer's scientific knowledge and ability, and at the same time it paradoxically knits together two conflicting sides of his persona—his denial of his roots in Grace and his recognition of those roots in his daughters.

His hobby is photography, but it takes a rather peculiar form. As Codi sees it, he takes and develops pictures of things that look like other things, such as clouds which could be seen as animals. He finally explains that his procedure actually is to try to find in his surroundings things that he can make look, in photographs, like images which he remembers from his past (259). This hobby, which he has pursued for a long time, suggests a merging in his mind of various realities. Things can look like other things, and as a result nothing is necessarily only what it seems to be. Alzheimer's disease removes from his consciousness a rational comprehension of thing seeming to merge with thing, and thus, past cannot be distinguished from present. This joining of the false and the true seems appropriate for a man who denies his background and the family from which he is descended and yet who returns to the place of that background and family to serve the very people who he feels treated him and his family like trash.

The other male character of significance in *Animal Dreams* is Loyd Peregrina, Codi's lover briefly in high school, the father of her miscarried baby, and soon after her return to Grace, her lover again. Of Native American origins, he is comfortable with his life in Grace, his family ties in Santa Rosalia Pueblo, his work on the railroad, and his hobby of cockfighting. In high school, he had been an important and admired person, and Codi had been surprised that he briefly, for a month, took notice of her. In her mind, his dropping her after that month is connected with her loss of the baby and with her sense of unworthiness. In Loyd's mind, his dropping her is an example of his being "a jerk," and he eventually apologizes to her for it (131). He now sees his behavior as having been thoughtless and cruel, and he is aware of having hurt a number of people. Codi, in her usual insecure way, is surprised that he even remembers her and relieved that he has no knowledge about her pregnancy. He, on the other hand, an Indian from an outlying place, felt below the daughter of the town doctor. Their perceptions, as so often happens in Kingsolver's worlds, do not match.

Always accompanied by his half-coyote dog Jack and with the reputation as an expert at cockfighting, Loyd is still a man who stands out. The cockfighting plot, which picks up the animal motif so prominent in the novel, is important for what it reveals about the region and culture of the place as well as for its significance for Loyd's character. Loyd's father had been a great master of this "sport," so Loyd had followed in the family footsteps. Arizona is specified as one of the few places where cockfighting is legal; therefore Loyd is not a lawbreaker for participating. Codi agrees to see a cockfight, apparently because she thinks she owes him that much, although she had been appalled at his involvement in what she sees as "kind of an unsavory business" (103).

The scene in which Codi observes her first and only cockfight (184–89) and its aftermath (189–91) is bloody and unpleasant. Information about types of fighting cocks ("gaffers" and "knifers") is conveyed, as is the amount of skill needed by the handler, who must manage his bird so that it continues the fight until it is either victorious or dead. The treatment of the birds, both the wounded winners and the dead losers, is horrific and appalls Codi. Her repulsion surprises Loyd, for whom this hobby has been simply a natural part of life. At first he defends his sport to her, pointing out that the roosters are bred for it, that a great skill is required on the part of the handler, and that death is just a part of life. Codi tries to explain that her attitude is not just sympathy for the birds but rather belief that people should not take pleasure in inflicting pain on other living beings (191). After some consideration, Loyd understands this new—to him—attitude; half an hour later he tells her that he will quit the sport. The most mature and open of the major characters, with the exception of Hallie, Loyd is able to examine other points of view and to adopt them when they seem right to him.

Oddly enough, Loyd, like Codi, has suffered a great loss, but his accommodation to his loss is very different from hers. He had had a twin brother, Leander, to whom he was very close; their relationship mirrors that of Codi and Hallie. Several images of their closeness demonstrate that the loss of Leander was no less important for Loyd than were Codi's losses for her. For example, when they visit the isolated area from which Loyd came, he shows her among all the ancient petroglyphs (rock carvings) a modern one of the clasped hands of two boys, clearly carved by and representing Loyd and Leander (216). Loyd's decision to give up cockfighting is connected to his memories of his brother's death in a bar fight, which Codi's comments have apparently made him see in a new light. In the half hour in which he makes the decision, he remarks to Codi that they are only fifteen miles from the place where Leander was killed by a drunk (191) and later he acknowledges that Leander's death was caused by "Puncture wounds. Internal hemorrhage" (209), the same kinds of wounds that cause the deaths of fighting cocks. His grief over his brother's death still is powerful enough to affect his actions, but for him the impact is good. It is significant that he gives up his sport for himself, not for Codi. Unlike Codi, he has not allowed his loss to cripple him emotionally. After Hallie's death, Loyd is able to use his loss of Leander in an attempt to comfort Codi, telling her that although she is changed by this great loss, she will be able to go on (309).

The reason that the loss of Leander was not the crippling blow to Loyd that the losses of her mother and baby were to Codi can be explained by the fact that unlike her he had a loving family and that he knew where he came from. Codi first identifies him as an Apache (52), but his tribal background is more complicated than that. He describes himself as a "mongrel," like his dog (91), with strains of Apache, Navajo, and Pueblo and the ability to speak all three of these Native American languages. But his real identification is as a Pueblo, with his mother's people, and it is to her home in the Santa Rosalia Pueblo that he takes Codi in an important chapter. His family home, presented through Codi's eyes, is idyllic, a great contrast to the emotionally starved household in which she had herself grown up. Loyd's mother, his aunt, his sisters, and a niece are present, all of them delighted to see Loyd and to meet her. Loyd is clearly deeply loved here and he loves these women who comprise his family. The household is a happy place, a mixture of Native American and Anglo culture, and Loyd's people delight in serving Codi their foods and introducing her to some of their customs. Loyd explains later that the culture is matrilineal, that is, "women are kind of the center of things up here. The man goes to the wife's place" (233). His father had never been an important part of his life. In a theme which Kingsolver was to pick up and develop further in *Pigs in Heaven*, that of acculturation or loss of culture, Loyd mentions that his father had been sent to a boarding school and separated from the "old ways" (233). Loyd, like Codi, had had an absent father, but unlike her had not been damaged by this fact. His losses of brother and father parallel hers of mother and baby in significance, but because he had retained a loving parent and a stable family life, the impact on him was less.

Loyd has given the same dedication to his profession on the railroad that he gave to the sport of cockfighting. Work on the railroad is about the only employment available in Grace, with the result that many of the men are often absent. When they are home, they spend much of their time wondering when they will get their next call to go out with a train. Loyd is accustomed to this life, and he is a skilled worker. When Codi finally listens to him talk about his work on the railroad, he explains to her the skill required and the danger involved in the apparently simple job of taking a long train down a hill, as well as his exhilaration at doing it exactly right (293–96). Throughout, in fact, Loyd reacts with appropriate emotion and behavior. Thus, when Codi finally tells him of her pregnancy and miscarriage, he is sad. She had not considered it any of his business, and yet when he knows about it, he grieves, too.

THEMATIC DEVELOPMENT

The central theme of *Animal Dreams*, that of how people become either detached or involved, plays out in complex ways. Most obvious are the contrasts between Codi and Hallie which form the basis of the novel, with Hallie, the absent sister, representing the point of view of the author. Also important is the treatment of Doc Homer, whose development into a distant father parallels Codi's becoming alienated from her feelings. Importantly, however, neither Codi nor Doc Homer remains as detached or alienated as the initial concept of the book would seem to suggest. From the very beginning, Doc Homer is shown to care deeply about his daughters, the implication being that it is because he loves them so deeply that he fears being hurt again as profoundly as he had been at his wife's death. He does show his love for the girls in strange ways, most oddly in his insistence that they wear the orthopedic shoes which they bitterly hate. His motivation is his concern for their feet and thus for their health, but they see the shoes only as one more way in which they are different from the rest of the people of Grace, another symbol of their being outsiders.

Codi, too, is not as detached as she believes. She does not have the courage or the desire to go to Central America, but she does return to Grace to find out what is happening to the father with whom she has such a distant relationship. Although she had not taken the final steps to qualify as a doctor, she saves a child's life when he nearly chokes. Despite her checkered work history—everything from working in convenience stores to posing for artists—she becomes an effective and innovative teacher in the one year that she is willing to allow herself at Grace High School. It is she who, with her pupils, discovers that the waters are polluted and lacking all microscopic life, and she indirectly sets into motion the campaign of the Stitch and Bitch Club to save Grace. Although she resists involvement in parts of that campaign, she does take an active role in it. But she always holds back to some degree, and until the end of the novel she considers herself too weak or incapable to make any difference. Her cynicism about the possibility that people can make a difference handicaps her.

Related to the theme of involvement and detachment is that of identity. Hallie always knew exactly who she was as well as what she wanted to do. Codi was less secure about her identity, a lack that is made overt in her discoveries about her ancestry. Considering herself always an outsider to Grace, she discovers that both her parents are actually natives of the community, her father primarily identified with the scorned Nolina family and her mother with an aristocratic Gracela line. On returning to the place she had never considered home, she finds that she really is at home there. She has a true friend in Emelina Domingos, she finds a lover in Loyd Peregrina, and she learns finally to understand her father and the deceits and concealments that have controlled his life. As a result of her discoveries and despite the crushing loss of Hallie, she is able to settle down in Grace, start her own family, and participate in the rituals of the community.

Another significant theme in *Animal Dreams* is that of relationships—both benign and hostile—with nature. Hallie, with her love for plants and her goal of teaching good crop-management techniques to people who desperately need that knowledge, is one strand. Codi, whose knowledge is mainly medical and physiological, demonstrates to her pupils the effects of pollution on the water and soil that give the orchards of Grace their life and the town its livelihood. Codi's attempts to prevent animal suffering—recall her distress over Loyd's cockfighting—are important and consistent; however, they are not always successful, as seen in her youthful efforts to save coyote pups and her mistaken attempt to rescue a peacock piñata.

Kingsolver's concern for ecology is ever present. Obvious is the negative depiction of the Black Mountain Mining Company and its uncaring pollution of the waters which it plans to cover up by building a dam and flooding the affected areas. Throughout the novel, a concern for care of land and animals is present. Loyd's Native American culture with its stress on harmony with Mother Earth and its pueblos that seem to grow from the land are other examples of how Kingsolver's ecological concerns are developed in the novel.

Also present in *Animal Dreams*, as is typical of Kingsolver's fiction, are some specifically political themes. Among them are Central American politics and U.S. involvement on the side of totalitarian and reactionary movements, and the shallow, dishonest press coverage of grassroots movements both in the United States and abroad. These themes are developed principally through the character of Hallie, her letters to Codi, and, after Hallie is kidnapped, Codi's campaign to publicize her sister's plight and achieve her release. Although crucial for the plot, these themes are less richly developed than some broader notions.

One such theme of particular interest, partly because of some comments Kingsolver has made on it, is that of violence. In an essay entitled, "Careful What You Let in the Door," she discusses her unsettled notions about the place of violence in fiction. Deeply opposed to censorship, she is also uncomfortable with much of the use of violence in contemporary fiction and film. In reading or seeing violence, she often feels "preyed upon" (*High Tide* 252). Her criteria for including violence in her fiction are that it must be an essential part of her story and that it must relate to the real world (*High Tide* 255). She goes on in the essay to discuss Hallie's offstage kidnapping and death as an example of such violence in her work, but surprisingly she does not mention the directly shown, very gory cockfighting scene. Both types of violence, however, meet her criteria of being essential to the particular fiction and truthful in reflecting actuality. Both are painful to read and thus both dramatize the horror of contemporary violence.

A FEMINIST READING OF *ANIMAL DREAMS*

Animal Dreams is a rich novel, including as it does a number of themes and a variety of characters. Many of the most interesting characters are women—Codi, Hallie, Emelina, and the women of the Stitch and Bitch Club come immediately to mind. All of these women are—or become—persons of strength who strive to change their realities. They become activists. In showing strong women as well as in examining the ways in which women are molded by their environments and experiences, *Animal Dreams* is a feminist novel.

Feminism in fiction can take a number of forms. Primarily, it is based on the equality of women and may dramatize ways in which they are discriminated against. Alternatively, a novel may illustrate women's capabilities to make valuable contributions to society. Most frequently the work either reveals ways in which women are influenced by their culture to become weak and, thus, are often victimized; or it dramatizes the experiences of strong women who become role models for others who are trying to achieve control over their lives and circumstances. Feminist novelists have made significant use of a reworked version of the *Bildungsroman*, as seen in *The Bean Trees*, to show women moving from weakness and victimization to strength. *Animal Dreams* does all of these things: Codi's weakness at the beginning of the novel combined with her growth and gradual maturation, Hallie's strength, and the political action of the women of the Stitch and Bitch Club are all aspects of the novel which are considered feminist.

Throughout the novel, Hallie is a positive feminist role model. Like many women of the 1980s, she acts on her political principles, travelling to Central America and risking her own life in order to do two things: to boycott the U.S. government which supported undemocratic political movements there, and to work directly with poor people who are suffering and dying in order to build better lives for their children. For Hallie, living by her beliefs is primary. Yet, she does not attempt to force her attitudes on others, telling Codi to find her own hopes and goals.

Similar observations can be made about other female characters in the novel. Once the women of the Stitch and Bitch Club understand what is happening to their town, they act. They are bright and inventive, making use of the materials and the skills they have—peacock feathers and the ability to make piñatas—to earn money for a campaign to save Grace from being destroyed. They work hard and with good humor as they make the piñatas and take them to Tucson to be sold on the street. Their work is recognized as folk art, and their artistic skills as well as their strength of character are demonstrated.

The women of the town, represented by Emelina, Codi's friend and landlady, Emelina's mother-in-law, Viola, and the members of the Stitch and Bitch Club, are much more prominent in the novel than are the men, with few exceptions. Doc Homer and Loyd are the only two males who play significant roles. But Doc Homer is an old man in failing health, no longer able to carry on his old function of caring for the people of Grace. Loyd is often absent, working for the railroad. In addition, he is not quite a native of Grace, being a Native American whose true roots are in the Santa Rosalia Pueblo. It is the women who keep things going and who, when needed, step forward to save their homes.

Kingsolver's experience researching and then writing *Holding the Line* has been particularly useful to her in creating *Animal Dreams* as a feminist novel. The villages she visited and came to know as she studied the

Phelps Dodge mine strike are similar to Grace, with its polluting mine company. The women whom she met in Morenci and Ajo are, with their strong Mexican-American heritage, much like the women of Grace. The absence of the men from the Phelps Dodge strike (for practical purposes—the need to find work) is echoed in the lesser presence of men in *Animal Dreams*, where many of the men are off working for the railroad much of the time and thus absent from the daily life of the village. *Holding the Line* is a nonfictional study of women from a very conservative culture finding their voices and making a difference. *Animal Dreams* dramatizes in fiction the way in which very similar women go through much the same process.

5

Pigs in Heaven
(1993)

Because it centers around characters already familiar from *The Bean Trees* and picks up their story three or four years later (Kingsolver said four in a 1993 interview [Perry 164], although the ages given for Turtle in the two books suggest three), *Pigs in Heaven* is considered a sequel to the earlier novel. Additionally, *Pigs in Heaven* ties up one very important plot line from *The Bean Trees*. In *The Bean Trees*, the ending finds Taylor Greer returning to Tucson with her now adopted daughter Turtle, confident that because she has legalized their relationship no one can take the child from her. However, the adoption is achieved through fraudulent means. Taylor's friends have posed as Turtle's birth parents, lying about their relationship with Turtle in order to relinquish the rights over her which they do not legally have. The happy ending of the earlier book, therefore, is based on deceit. But that book gives no indication that this will be a problem for Taylor and Turtle. Taylor has been unable to find Turtle's actual parents and has simply done the best she could in that situation. While the ending of *The Bean Trees* is emotionally satisfying in terms of the novel, it does leave some uncertainty about the security of the relationship between Taylor and Turtle and thus a ready opening for a sequel which will make use of the instability caused by the legal fraud. Kingsolver has said that some time after the publication of *The Bean Trees* she "realized with embarrassment that I had completely neglected a whole moral area when I wrote about this Native American kid being swept off the reservation and raised by a very loving white mother. It was something I hadn't thought about, and I felt I needed to make that right in another book" (Perry 165).

Kingsolver has resisted the identification of *Pigs in Heaven* as a sequel and the later novel certainly can stand alone as an independent work. The two books have important differences in method and presentation as they advance the story of their central characters. *Pigs in Heaven* continues some themes and settings as well as characters from the earlier story, but it also adds themes and settings, and some of its most interesting characters are new.

The question with which Kingsolver began *Pigs in Heaven* concerns the relationship between the individual and the community, specifically relating to differing beliefs about the importance of each. People living in the Southwest are familiar with cases of well-meaning white families adopting Native American infants who are later wanted back by their tribes. The white families plead the child's best interest: How can it be in the best interest of the child to be removed from the only parents he or she has ever known? On the other hand, the Native Americans plead the best interest of the tribe: How can it be in the best interest of the tribe to lose the children who are its very future? A related issue is the question of how it can be in the best interest of children to lack knowledge of the culture of their birth, particularly since they clearly reveal their Native American background in their appearance and their appearance will almost certainly lead to racial discrimination against them. The basic question is that of varying values—individual against community. This question is considered most directly through the controversy over Native American children being adopted outside their tribes. By obvious extension, this theme is yet another depiction of the values of community and the ways people help each other—becoming active participants in others' lives—that Kingsolver has considered in her preceding novels.

STRUCTURE AND PLOT DEVELOPMENT

The action of *Pigs in Heaven* is divided into three sections, each entitled according to a season of the year. The ironic opening occurs in spring, the season of rebirth and new beginnings, and upsets the stability established at the end of *The Bean Trees*. Even more ironic, it opens on Easter weekend, with a character's near death on Saturday and his rescue and return to life on Monday. This is not a literal death and resurrection, the character in question is far from a Christ figure, and the events do not quite occur on Good Friday (the date of Jesus's death) and Easter (His resurrection). Although the timing of the action as well as its nature clearly relate these events to the Easter story, this version is askew in just about all respects. Lucky Buster, who falls over the spillway at Hoover Dam, is a middle-aged retarded man, and his fall occurs because he is trying to pick up a discarded soda pop can. His motives may be good, although they are a bit crazy, but his action is in no sense sacrificial. Nor is his return to life meaningful in any particular way. This resurrection in this spring of rebirth has the unintended and indirect consequences of nearly causing the breaking of Taylor Greer's parental relationship with her adopted daughter Turtle. This occurs because of their good deed, Lucky's rescue, over the protests of lazy security workers. The novel thus is set into motion by ironies. This is a spring of danger, not of joy.

"Spring" creates the conflict of the plot by raising the issue of Turtle's adoption. It brings Taylor and Annawake Fourkiller, representatives of the two opposing points of view, into contact with each other and thus poses Kingsolver's central question quite specifically, more specifically and directly than the issues of either *The Bean Trees* or *Animal Dreams* have been presented. Taylor takes Turtle and flees, attempting to evade the issue and also repeating the journey motif of *The Bean Trees*. In fact, this section even has a circular structure, for the rescue set at Hoover Dam occurs within the first few pages, and the action takes Taylor and Turtle back to that same setting at the end.

The second and third sections follow chronologically and are entitled "Summer" and "Fall." In "Summer," characters important to the plot are introduced or reintroduced as Taylor's aimless flight continues. Taylor's mother, called Mama in Taylor's first-person narration of *The Bean Trees* but referred to as Alice in the omniscient narrative of *Pigs in Heaven*, has briefly appeared in the opening chapter of this novel and now enters as a major character in her own right. She flies west to join Taylor. Cash Stillwater, who along with Alice will figure in an important subplot and in the novel's conclusion, is introduced. Sugar Hornbuckle, Alice's cousin, who will be an instrument drawing together the major characters of the book, has been mentioned in the earlier novel but now appears as a character in her own right. In this section, the conflict continues, even while the reader, by fitting information about the characters together, realizes that there may be a possible solution which would enable both Taylor's maternal cause and the tribe's communal needs to be satisfied at the same time.

The final section, "Fall," is set partly in Seattle, where Taylor has fled, partly in Oklahoma, where all the characters and plot lines are joined. It brings a solution to the adoption issue, which is the novel's embodiment of Kingsolver's examination of issues of individual and community. This solution may be seen either as bringing about a fortunate compromise which will leave both sides happy or as being based on a gigantic and unbelievable coincidence. Again the irony of the seasons is apparent. Fall is usually the time of fruition and of awareness of the approaching death which is winter. But in this novel, fall is the time of new beginnings. It brings a beginning for Alice and Cash. It brings a partial reestablishment, now on legal grounds, of the parent-child relationship of Taylor and Turtle, and it brings the beginning of a connection between Turtle and her birth family as well as the tribal culture from which she comes.

The plot progresses in gradual steps, following the movements of major characters, principally Taylor and Alice, as they travel from place to place, either seeking to avoid the issue of Turtle's placement with Taylor or to move toward a solution of this problem. The novel opens with Alice, setting up her dissatisfaction with her marriage and establishing her willingness to leave her husband quickly when her daughter needs her. Through her memories, the opening chapter also introduces Alice's second cousin Sugar and Alice's awareness that Sugar is living in Oklahoma as a Cherokee. Although readers of *The Bean Trees* know of Alice's Cherokee connection, this relationship is not yet introduced in *Pigs in Heaven*. In the second chapter of the novel, the action quickly shifts to Hoover Dam, which Taylor and Turtle are visiting while on a brief vacation. It is here that the inciting incident, the episode which sets into motion the action of the novel and which Kingsolver has described as "just one of those fluky things that happen in my novels" (Perry 164), occurs. Turtle happens to be the only one to see the accident which sends Lucky Buster, an adult but retarded man, over the spillway and out of sight. Turtle, still a preschooler, does not realize the significance of what she has seen and only later tells her mother, who shows the usual maternal skepticism about the literal truth of her daughter's story. When she is certain that Turtle is telling the truth, they return to the dam and, with some difficulties because it is Easter weekend and the security staff is not well equipped to understand and act upon such an emergency, they are able to set a search into motion so that Lucky Buster is rescued.

The ensuing news coverage leads to Turtle's being asked to appear on an Oprah Winfrey talk-show segment about children who save lives. That television appearance, seen by Annawake Fourkiller, a Cherokee lawyer who recognizes Turtle as Cherokee, leads to questions about the legality of Turtle's placement with Taylor. At this point, the complications of the plot are set up, and what follows grows from the issues that Annawake raises and from Taylor's reaction to them. In brief, then, the plot moves forward in the following major steps: Taylor flees with Turtle, and they travel to Las Vegas and then Seattle, where Taylor hopes to find anonymity and safety for herself and her daughter. Alice joins her daughter and granddaughter, seeking to support them emotionally as well as financially (though her resources are slim). Going to Oklahoma, Alice uses her old connection with Sugar, hoping to find out about tribal attempts to regain Turtle's custody. Persuaded that Annawake, whom they had seen as an enemy, really is not a complete antagonist, Alice persuades Taylor and Turtle to come to Oklahoma. Once all the major characters are in Cherokee lands, the plot winds rather quickly to its conclusion, bringing a solution to the dilemma of Turtle's situation, torn between the only parent she knows and the family and tribe who are strangers to her.

Each step of the plot—its setting and the characters present—is fully developed and credible, with a richness of texture bringing life and vitality. Each step of the plot also follows logically from the one preceding it, although the final solution rests on coincidence. Thus, although the reader foresees something of what the conclusion will be, it still may seem somewhat less than believable. This relates to the task which Kingsolver had set herself. She had selected an issue, that of adoptions of Native American children outside their people, which is complex and troubling, to which there are no easy answers and about which there is no consensus in our society. Arguments for both positions on this issue are emotionally and legally compelling. She was seeking to dramatize this issue by using characters many of whom were already known to and loved by a wide public. There is no wise King Solomon here to discover a right answer, and the conflict is between a mother and a people, not between two women. The wisdom needed is more profound than that exemplified in the biblical story, although that story is referred to by characters seeking a nonconfrontational solution. While there is no easy answer for these characters in this situation, the novel comes to what is perhaps the most fortunate balance possible. Kingsolver's persistent optimism, voiced in the novel's opening chapter from Alice's point of view as her marriage is dissolving, expresses well the feeling of the novel's ending, that rational and loving people can work things out. Therefore, "No matter what kind of night you're having, morning always wins" (6).

NARRATIVE METHOD

The choice of the question about the relationship between individualism and community, with particular reference to the issue of Native American children adopted by white families, presented Kingsolver with some crucial problems in the construction of the novel. Since *Pigs in Heaven* would be read by a predominantly white and middle-class audience, the sympathies of readers would naturally tilt in the direction of individualism, of the child's best interest. Kingsolver's goal is to balance the two sides of the question so that, even though their sympathies would most easily lie on the side of the individual, readers would see that both arguments were right. This problem is made even more difficult to solve by the fact that many readers would also be already familiar with and fond of Taylor and Turtle from *The Bean Trees* and would automatically find themselves empathizing with them, seeing any characters arguing the tribal position as the novel's antagonists (those opposing the protagonist). Thus, balancing the scales so that readers would not only understand but even sympathize with the tribal point of view required careful planning.

Kingsolver uses two major methods of trying to balance the two sides of the question of individual and community. One is through the creation of a complex and interesting character to represent the tribal side, the character of Annawake Fourkiller, to be discussed later. The other method, more subtle but no less important, is the choice of the omniscient method of narration. The omniscient point of view is distinguished from the limited method in that the story is told as if by a godlike narrator who knows, sees, and is capable of telling everything about all of the characters. The narrative thus is not limited to the knowledge and experience of any one of the characters. This method is different from that used for *The Bean Trees*, in which most of the story is narrated by Taylor herself and thus is seen almost completely from her point of view. In *Pigs in Heaven*, the narrative method does not automatically favor any of the characters by placing the reader's perceptions within those of that character, as had been done in *The Bean Trees* and also in *Animal Dreams*.

Here individualism, as represented by Taylor, and community values, as shown in Annawake, are seen equally from the perspective of an outside, all-knowing narrative voice. That voice is able to take the reader into the thoughts and feelings of both Taylor and Annawake, so that their logical arguments and the emotional bases for those arguments can be known and balanced against each other. This choice is one which Kingsolver made quite consciously. She pointed out in a television interview shown on Public Broadcasting System that she had difficulty in finding examples in contemporary American fiction of the use of the omniscient method and thus had to search widely for models ("Barbara Kingsolver," PBS *Signature* series).

The omniscient method is particularly appropriate for this novel since the action occurs in several varied locales and among differing groups of characters. It is only near the end of the novel that the various plot strands are woven together. The point of view of no single character could be used since no one character is present throughout the action, and the omniscient method enables the author to tell all of the stories which will come together. The other possibility (more similar to the method used in the early chapters of *The Bean Trees* and to that of *Animal Dreams* as well as the method she uses later in *The Poisonwood Bible*) would have been to vary the narrative method according to the plot line and characters of the particular portion of the story. Additionally, the change from Taylor's first-person narrative for most of *The Bean Trees* to the omniscient storytelling of *Pigs in Heaven* helps to break some patterns established in the earlier novel. Separation from Taylor, which implies sympathy with other characters, is instrumental in lowering Taylor and her point of view so that they are not automatically seen as most central to the novel. In fact, Taylor is not present for large portions of the action and therefore could not have narrated the whole story.

It must be recognized, however, that Kingsolver's attempts to play fair and to balance the sides of her chosen issue are not completely successful. The largest portion of the narrative follows either Taylor or her mother, who is working to enable Taylor to keep custody of Turtle. Though readers are taken inside Annawake's consciousness and come to understand and sympathize with her point of view, she never becomes as living a character as Taylor. This, in addition to many readers' already existing fondness for Taylor and Turtle and the predisposition on the part of white middle-class readers to value individualism and the best interests of the child, means that the balance is not truly maintained. At the end of the novel, typical readers will most likely be hoping for any solution which will leave Taylor and Turtle together. But Annawake's position and her arguments for the tribal point of view have been established as serious and worth consideration. Both Alice and Taylor acknowledge this.

CHARACTER DEVELOPMENT

Two striking characters in this novel, Barbie and Jax, are not really important for plot or the central thematic development. They are colorful and interesting, however—one of the reasons that Kingsolver's work, teeming with similarly fascinating characters, appeals to a wide audience. Barbie is a particularly vivid example. She is a caricature of certain notions of contemporary femininity, having consciously made herself into a living Barbie doll. She considers the fact that her birth name was Barbara a sign that she was intended to become a human incarnation of the doll, and she has gone so far as to change her name simply to "Barbie," with no last name but with a tiny symbol, an encircled "TM" for "trademark," appended to her signature. Her clothing really consists of costumes. Her physical measurements approach but do not equal those which a full-sized Barbie doll would have (she can't quite manage to slim her waist far enough to simulate the toy's incredible hourglass figure). Her makeup is always thick and dramatic, and she is constantly touching it up. She is cheerful, with the perkiness which she believes the living doll would have, and she is a walking encyclopedia of knowledge about the various models of the doll manufactured over the years. Her speech, sprinkled with "like" as, for instance, in "I'm like, why not? You know?" (134), echoes popular speech of teenagers of the time. She considers making herself into Barbie to be her career, and waiting on tables in restaurants is just what she does to support herself while she is trying to figure out some way to make a living from being Barbie. All of this is comic as well as being satiric of the image of women both reflected and supported by the popular toy.

The more ominous side of making an ideal out of such an unrealistic vision of womanhood is shown in both subtle and not-so-subtle ways. Subtly, it is hinted that Barbie may be bulimic, when Alice notices that she always goes to the bathroom immediately after eating something (161), though neither Alice nor Taylor draws any immediate conclusions about this behavior. Taylor realizes Barbie's bulimia only much later (325). More obviously, Barbie's ethics are, to say the least, weak. Having pitied her and felt responsible for unintentionally causing Barbie to lose her job as a waitress in a casino restaurant, Taylor and Alice allow her to travel with them, although they find her wearing as a traveling companion. They lose their pity for her when they discover that the purse she carries with her at all times is full of coins she has stolen from the casino. Later Taylor learns that Barbie unashamedly passes currency that she has printed on a color copier. This discovery enables Taylor to distance herself and Turtle from Barbie without any guilt feelings. Barbie's presence in the plot does not move it forward nor does she significantly contribute to the development of major themes of the novel. But she adds comedy to the book and provides a satire of one aspect of American popular culture.

Jax, although he is a less prominent character than Barbie, is more important to the novel because of his relationship with Taylor. He and Taylor are lovers, living together while Lou Ann Ruiz, Taylor's housemate in *The Bean Trees*, lives with the man she has found at the end of the earlier novel. The close friendship between the two young women continues, and Lou Ann appears briefly several times throughout *Pigs in Heaven*. Jax is a rock musician, a peaceful, easygoing, and nurturing man. He loves Taylor and is far more dependent on her than she is on him. He lives in and through his music. Despite his love for Taylor and his longing to make their relationship more permanent than it seems to be, he is unfaithful to Taylor with Gundi, their eccentric artist landlady, while Taylor is gone. Greatly regretting his betrayal of Taylor, he insists on telling her of his lapse because he feels deeply that their relationship must be built on honesty if it is to have any value. His confession, made during one of their telephone calls while Taylor and Turtle are fleeing, seems at first not to affect Taylor greatly, but his honesty does affect her decision at the end of the novel to make their relationship more permanent, perhaps even through marriage. Offstage throughout much of the novel, Jax nevertheless provides a secure home base for both Taylor and Turtle to remember and to hope to return to.

Alice Stamper Greer, Taylor's mother, kept offstage throughout *The Bean Trees* where she is referred to as "Mama," becomes an important and very vivid character in *Pigs in Heaven*. The later novel opens with Alice as she is thinking about her unfulfilling marriage to Harland, whom she had wed hopefully at the end of the preceeding book. Harland is more interested in his collection of old automobile headlights and in watching television than in talking with her. At the age of sixty-one, she doesn't have any clear notion of what else she wants to do, but she dreams of something better. When Taylor is in trouble, Alice seizes the opportunity to leave Harland and fly (her first flight ever) to Las Vegas to join her daughter and granddaughter as they try to evade legal problems. Alice is warm and open, making friends as easily as her daughter. Her heart is caring and loyal, but her head is clear. She is able to understand Annawake's notions of justice for Turtle and the tribe. Her openness to new experiences enables her to easily establish relationships with the Cherokees and is essential to her sometimes bemused but usually approving introduction to their culture. She begins as Taylor's emissary to the tribe and becomes an instrument in the gradual coming together of Taylor and Turtle's birth family.

Two characters who are secondary in some senses but crucial for the forward movement of the plot are Sugar and Cash. Sugar, Alice's second cousin with whom she shares a Cherokee ancestry and to whom she had been close as a child in rural Mississippi, serves basic plot functions in that she is Alice's obvious link to the Cherokee world. Alice had always been aware of—and had impressed upon Taylor—the fact that their Cherokee forebears give them a potential claim upon the Cherokee Nation if they ever choose to press it. This much was established in *The Bean Trees*. In *Pigs in Heaven*, Sugar's presence in Oklahoma, living now with the tribe from which Turtle is descended, becomes central. Ironically, however, Sugar's continuing presence there seems due more to her marriage to a Cherokee than to her own relatively diluted ancestry. Having had a non-Indian upbringing, she understands how tribal life may appear to an outsider, and she serves as a good guide for Alice, introducing her to the customs and values of the Cherokees. But she is also a vivid and appealing character in her own right.

Sugar had one brief but dramatic claim to fame. As a beautiful young woman living in Oklahoma, she had posed for a picture which had obtained national circulation, being published in *Life* magazine. The picture showed her with a sign welcoming travelers to her small Oklahoma town. In the picture, she is wearing a circlet of daisies in her hair and drinking from a can of soda pop as she leans against the sign, which reads, "Welcome to Heaven" (7). It is the town's odd name and the irony of a celestial name for a drab village in a dreary part of eastern Oklahoma which give comic punch to the picture. But it is Sugar's presence as the picture's human interest which causes it to be remembered years later by Alice from her home in Kentucky and by Sugar's friends and family in Oklahoma, although she is now a hearty and overweight grandmother, not the slim and lovely young woman of the picture.

Sugar is surrounded by grandchildren and friends. She is happy in her marriage and in her life in her community, and she feels no embarrassment about her changed appearance. She gleefully gathers poke leaves by the roadside, wanting them for salads, to the surprise of Alice who is startled by behavior she at first considers characteristic of shiftless poverty. She realizes, however, that Sugar sees the poke leaves as a part of her world, not owned by anyone in particular and available to anyone who may be able to make good use of them. Thus, Sugar's behavior helps Alice see something of the gulf in values between the Cherokee world of the oddly and yet appropriately named Heaven and the white culture which is all she has known.

Sugar serves as Alice's guide in a number of respects. She introduces her to people and explains the sometimes complicated relationships confronting her. For example, when Cash takes Alice to the stomp, a tribal affair that combines social and religious functions, Sugar explains much of the activity to her and persuades her to join in the dance. Sugar also interprets people's behavior for her. She points out that Cash cannot stay with Alice, as they are members of different clans because clan membership is matrilineal (it descends through the female line). She tells Alice of their mutual membership, through their grandmother, in the Bird Clan—something Alice had not known. Alice goes with Sugar to the Cherokee Heritage Center to her find her own family records, thus placing herself emotionally—and potentially legally—in the Cherokee Nation. Neither Alice's visit nor the final form of the solution to the dilemma about Turtle's placement could be worked out quite as they are without the presence of Alice in Oklahoma and in the plot of the novel.

Cash Stillwater, like Annawake Fourkiller and her Uncle Ledger Fourkiller, is a member of the Cherokee Nation and identifies himself as a Cherokee. Those three characters are the principal representatives of Native American culture in the novel, but they reveal different attitudes as well as different generations. Cash's and Annawake's life experiences are similar in some ways, as both are very aware of the process of acculturation—of being removed from the culture of their heritage—and both feel with justice that they have been victimized by it. Annawake is the expression of one side of the central issue of the novel and thus is almost as much symbol as character, while Cash is important to the movement of the plot.

As a member of the older generation and as a father and grandfather who has seen his family disintegrate, Cash is in some respects a beaten man. His wife has died an unpleasant death from cancer, and of his two daughters, one is dead, and the other "[m]ight as well be" (114). His infant granddaughter has disappeared. Disappointed and grief-stricken, he lives in Wyoming, where he makes a living by bagging groceries and by doing Indian beadwork, usually a woman's craft, which he had learned by watching the women of his family. His work thus is a strange blend of white and Indian worlds, and neither task brings him much pleasure. He does the beadwork to help Rose, his woman friend, who is employed to do beadwork while sitting in a storefront window where tourists can watch her. Ironically however, her beadwork is simpler and less interesting than his; he helps her out in the evenings by making items for her to take to her employer the next day. He is an outsider in Wyoming, and his dismay at seeing Rose on display as she hunches over her beadwork adds to his despair.

When he returns to his Cherokee world, he is at home and becomes more at peace with himself. He does two things which are important to the action of the novel. He inquires about the whereabouts of his missing granddaughter, Lacey, thus setting into motion tribal inquiries about the child who readers immediately know must be Turtle. This he does of his own choice. His other crucial action, into which he is not very subtly manipulated by Annawake, is setting out to court Alice. Like Sugar, he helps begin to integrate Alice into the life of the community, and his gentleness and quiet understanding, so different from the neglect of her husband, are deeply attractive to Alice. Their courtship and his final very public proposal of marriage help to create the possibilities of a final compromise about Turtle's placement which will satisfy both sides of the conflict.

The other characters, one major and one minor, who represent the Cherokee world and its attitudes and values are Annawake Fourkiller, who is also central to the plot, and Annawake's Uncle Ledger, who is minor in the plot but serves important symbolic functions. Uncle Ledger appears in two ways; as the foster parent who reared Annawake and whom she loves and respects, and as the medicine chief who is revered by the community and who takes an important role in the ritual of the stomp in a critical scene. His aloof dignity and pride and the awe with which he is always treated indicate his importance as man and as symbol. When Annawake's birth family was broken up, in a way typical of the time and place, he took her in and trained her to become an "ambassador" for her people. He encouraged her to learn and made her speak English. He himself remains deeply imbedded in his own culture, and at the stomp he is the one who lights the ceremonial pipe which then is passed among the assembled people. Less seriously, he performs more mundane functions in the community, as, for example, when he is called away to bless a new truck (277). Secular and spiritual are closely connected in this Cherokee world, a principle demonstrated through the character of Uncle Ledger.

Annawake, Ledger's ambassador to the white world who practices law as her method of aiding her people, is as deeply wounded as Cash, and her hurt helps to explain her intentness on just treatment for the tribe. Fortunately, she is able to rise above her pain and understand nontribal attitudes as well as to sympathize with Taylor's and Turtle's deep attachment to each other. She, like Cash, comes from a broken family, but her response to her deep pain is to try to do something about it. Having lost a twin brother, Gabriel, to adoption into the white world and having seen his inability to survive there, she is personally and emotionally committed to returning lost children to their tribes. But she is also an intelligent and sensitive young woman, able to see other points of view. Kingsolver uses her to express the Native American position on adoptions out of the tribe, to explain Cherokee culture and values, and to convey little lessons in the history of the Cherokee. Kingsolver is just as skillful here as she is in *The Bean Trees* in integrating information into the plot, and it is evidence of the author's mastery that those scenes are readable and interesting, moving the action forward and giving information as the reader needs it in order to understand the behavior of the characters. Annawake's position as the antagonist to Taylor's protagonist predisposes readers to see her as the enemy, but she is a likeable character and her truths are convincingly presented. The fact that Annawake, despite her deep commitment to justice for her people, is able to sympathize with other points of view makes her a particularly effective spokesperson for her own beliefs.

Taylor and Turtle, the two characters with whom readers most empathize, are several years older than they were in *The Bean Trees*, but they have little changed. The discussions of these characters in the examination of the earlier novel remain accurate here as well. Being a small child, Turtle has changed more than Taylor has. In *Pigs in Heaven* she enters first grade while mother and daughter are in Seattle. Closely bonded with Taylor, she is a charming child, who only occasionally reveals any continuing impact of the abuse she suffered as an infant. Withdrawal into herself is still her method of coping when she becomes particularly upset, but now Taylor is able to see the beginning stages of the withdrawal and sometimes can stave it off by distracting Turtle's attention to other things. Parallel to the revelation late in *The Bean Trees* that Turtle had seen her mother buried is her quick recognition of Cash as her beloved "Pop-pop" when first she sees him (321). That recognition, similar to recognition scenes as old as those in Greek tragedy, makes her identification as his granddaughter finally clear. This memory is a happy one and indicates that abused as she was, her babyhood was not completely appalling. One minor detail is the revelation that Turtle's birth name was actually Lacey, not April, as Taylor had concluded in *The Bean Trees*. This discrepancy, or alteration in the author's conception of the character, is not explained. She is a well-characterized five- or six-year-old child, and it might be noted that the author mentions in her acknowledgments her daughter's contribution to the novel as the one "who gave me five-year-old insights and reasons to keep writing." However, Camille Kingsolver, the writer's older daughter, is at pains to deny that she was a model for Turtle in any of the odd details of Turtle's life and background ("Barbara Kingsolver," PBS *Signature* series).

To the analysis of Taylor provided earlier need be added only comment on the depths of her love for Turtle and her willingness to sacrifice for the child. This quality appears in several ways. Taylor must make difficult financial choices while they are living in Seattle and she is supporting them by working at low-paying jobs. Sometimes this means the choice of which monthly bill to pay. When fall comes, school clothes for Turtle become a major priority, and Taylor lets other bills go unpaid in order to provide Turtle with outfits that will not be too different from those worn by the other children. (That Turtle is not an idealized version of childhood is shown by her whining that her clothes are not quite like those worn by the others, whom she wants to like her.) More significantly, near the end of the novel, Taylor has some doubts about her ability to be the mother Turtle needs. This doubt is inspired in part by her learning that Turtle is lactose intolerant. Like many people of non-Caucasian racial background, she cannot tolerate milk and milk products. This likelihood was pointed out to Taylor by Annawake in their first meeting. Partly because of anger at this stranger, who she fears may try to take Turtle away from her, lecturing her about how to care for her child, Taylor insists that Turtle drink milk and will not believe that Turtle does not like ice cream. When she learns that Turtle's persistent stomach cramps are in fact the result of the milk she has obediently been drinking, Taylor is horrified that she has unintentionally harmed her child. Thus, she becomes dubious for a time about her motherhood of Turtle being in the child's best interests. Their mutual love and bonding is so great that she continues to struggle to keep Turtle with her. It is with some reluctance that she accepts the compromise which will send Turtle to live with Cash for several months each year and which makes him the child's legal guardian, though still allowing Taylor joint custody.

SETTINGS

Settings in *Pigs in Heaven* are varied, ranging through much of the far western United States. Several of these locales, particularly Tucson and Oklahoma, are repetitive of *The Bean Trees*, though there are significant differences. Tucson now is Taylor's established home, and her situation there is a little different from what it is in the earlier book. The main differences are the changes worked by the passage of several years: Lou Ann and Taylor no longer share a house, each of them now living happily with a lover. Tucson itself is unchanged.

The treatment of Oklahoma, however, is quite different. In the earlier novel, Oklahoma is mainly a place to travel through or to get away from. Taylor associates it with boring flatness and aridity, as well as with the abuse that Turtle had suffered. She returns there only for the most pressing legal reasons. The view of Oklahoma, particularly of the Cherokee Nation, provided in *Pigs in Heaven* is different. Here it is shown to be a varied world. There is poverty and ignorance, but there are also hills and wooded areas where people live in harmony and have created true community. Alice serves as the eyes and sensibility to which this new picture is presented. Her experiences with the people—first Sugar and then all those she meets through Sugar—show her that in this community the values of family, including a widely extended concept of family, are treasured. She sees adolescent boys and girls who behave respectfully toward their elders and observes a way of life in which sharing is taken for granted. The stomp, with its dual spiritual and social aspects, helps to integrate Alice into the community. It occurs in a particularly holy place, a wooded area which is similar to the landscape of the southeastern United States from which the Cherokees were removed a century and a half earlier. Central to the events at the stomp is the presence of the sacred fire which had been brought from the Southeast on the Trail of Tears and carefully preserved ever since. Place and fire join with dance to enable a deeply spiritual expression, and people of all ages and both sexes join in. Secular and worldly are joined, also, as the evening contains elements of both worship and fun. As a people torn from ancestral lands, the community is still able to create a new homeland, while never forgetting the old, and live in harmony with nature and each other in an environment which could have only been seen as hostile.

Other locales, less significant, are also necessary for the plot and are vividly and effectively depicted. Chief among them are: Hoover Dam where the rescue which sets the plot in motion occurs; Las Vegas to which Taylor flees and which she sees as garish and unnatural; Seattle where she lives for a time and which is presented accurately as a city of varied landscapes and opportunities; and Wyoming where Cash unhappily whiles away his exile and regrets the treatment of Indians as tourist attractions. Also worth notice is the presentation of the Oprah Winfrey show, which is located in Chicago, but the city is not fully developed. Instead, Kingsolver concentrates on the show itself, on the glitter and basic dishonesty of television. The concern for the makeup and clothing of guests on the show is satirically presented, with the telling detail that it doesn't matter whether their clothing fits since it may be pinned up in back. After all, the sloppy alterations won't show on camera. Only the surface matters in the glitzy world of television.

THEME

The central theme of *Pigs in Heaven* is the conflict between white middle-class values of individualism and Native American values of community and tradition. Each of these sets of values is personified in a single character and is dramatized through the custody battle over Turtle. Taylor represents the general American value of individualism as it relates to "the best interest of the child"—the phrase used in adoption and child custody cases. Annawake represents the values of the tribe, with tribal consciousness of historical attempts to destroy the Cherokee people and culture and of long-lasting efforts to keep tribe, culture, and language alive. While in the process of writing *Pigs in Heaven*, Kingsolver described the novel as being "about characters who have an extreme conflict of interest, and there is no way to resolve it to the complete satisfaction of them both.... And both sides have a point" (Perry 154).

As in *The Bean Trees*, the most important themes are developed both through dramatization and discussion, with specific and detailed information presented. A series of scenes centering around Annawake as the representative of tribal values is central to this development. Annawake has two important functions. She is the lawyer who may remove Turtle from her home with Taylor and who thus sets the plot in motion, but she is also a spokesperson who presents historical and cultural information. Through her, information is conveyed about the 1838 Trail of Tears, when Cherokees were cruelly marched from their ancestral homes in the East, which were desired by white farmers, to arid lands in Oklahoma, which no one else wanted, with many dying on the way. She also relays instructive information about adoptions in which a third of Cherokee children are lost to the tribe and to their extended families. She is the one who succinctly expresses the conflict between Native and white values, between the group or community, on one side, and the individual, on the other, as this conflict applies to the question of adoptions out of the tribe. From her and her pain over the breakup of her family—especially over the loss of her twin brother Gabriel who was adopted into the white world where he never fit in, turned to a life of crime, and is eventually incarcerated in Leavenworth Prison—comes information about the continuing effects of ill-treatment of Native Americans. She explains to Alice the process of acculturation that has destroyed so many lives and families, describing the boarding schools that enforce use of English and make young people strangers to their own language and culture (227).

Other sources are also used to convey information. For example, Sugar tells Alice that many Cherokees had been robbed of their land allotments in Oklahoma. This helps explain the poverty prevailing there. She is able to point out one relatively prosperous house along a road, identifying it as the property of a white couple (194). Sugar also takes Alice to the Cherokee Heritage Center and helps her learn more about the tribe's history and trace her connection to it. The scene in which the stomp is directly presented dramatizes an important element of Cherokee life and culture.

The picture that emerges is of a tragic history of a proud people, which Kingsolver summarizes movingly in a conversation between Annawake and Alice. Kingsolver manages to pack a great deal of historical information, movingly detailed, into a few brief pages (278–85). Prominent here is the story of the Trail of Tears which tells how the Cherokee were torn away from the lands where they felt a connection to the universe and consequently created their own Nation in Oklahoma, with their own schools and written language, which Annawake regrets that she never learned to read. All these accomplishments were then taken from them, partly by theft and deceit, when others saw possibilities in the "useless" land the Cherokee had been given, and partly through official actions.

The government boarding schools, which enforced the use of English, created a generation which was alienated from its language and culture. Annawake's mother had been one of those. Annawake thinks of her as a "die-trying acculturated Cherokee, like most of her generation, who chose the Indian Baptist Church over stomp dances and never wore moccasins in her life" (59). She also was pregnant at sixteen, bore five sons and a daughter, abused alcohol, and while still only thirty-five was placed in an institution, leading to the breakup of her family. This family history parallels that of Cash Stillwater, one of his daughters giving birth to a child, Turtle, in a car and committing suicide in the same or another car. The other daughter, caring for Turtle, has a boyfriend who abuses her and the child, which she gives away, perhaps in a moment of hope that anything else will be better than what the child is suffering. This second daughter is also completely estranged from her father.

From all of this background, the reason for the Indian Child Welfare Act, which requires permission of the tribe, not just of the individual birth parent, before a child may be adopted out of the tribe, becomes comprehensible. Annawake calls what has happened to Native Americans a "holocaust" (281), and the desperate need for tribes to retain custody of their children in order to survive becomes clear. The plight of Turtle and Taylor's yearning to retain custody of her seem insignificant in the light of this suffering and need.

Considering the suffering the Cherokees have undergone, their openness and acceptance of outsiders are striking. Contrasting with the racial discrimination which Native Americans—including those adopted into white families—suffer, is the ease with which many outsiders are accepted into the tribe. True, there are requirements of certain ancestral connections to the tribe, but once having proof of such descent, one need simply ask to be "enrolled." Alice, with a Cherokee grandmother, has that right, and Sugar, with the same rather diluted ancestry, lives as a valued member of the community. As Annawake emphasizes, being a Cherokee is more a matter of shared culture than of blood, a "mind-set" (275) which is more essential than biological connections.

The theme of conflicting values regarding individual and community is examined in very complex ways. Most obvious is the conflict over the adoption of Turtle, in which staying with Taylor would be best for her as an individual and returning to the tribe would be best for the tribe, the community. In addition, paralleling this conflict is the contrast between Native American and white popular culture. For the Native Americans the community is primary, and, in part, it is this sense of the tribe's importance that is lost for the generation which was acculturated by its removal to the government boarding schools. For white culture, the rights of the individual receive primary value. This difference in values, in automatic assumptions about what is good, makes it difficult for Cherokee and white to understand each other. Simply coming to understand that there are other ways to look at the world is a big step forward first for Alice and then for Taylor. The novel implies that the two value systems are incompatible, although each is right in some respects. It does not specifically appraise one as being more worthy than the other but rather suggests that each has its place and meaning for its people—and that tearing any such value system from its people is likely to lead to disaster. Nevertheless, the novel dramatically demonstrates that the Cherokee's community values offer strengths lacking in Western stress on individualism.

For Kingsolver, the Western notion of individualism is connected to the optimistic American assumption that if one just works hard enough, success will follow automatically. This belief is part of the so-called American dream, the assurance that anyone can succeed in this country if only he or she will put forth enough effort. Kevin, an acquaintance of Taylor's in Seattle, puts forth this conviction in blunt and almost cruel terms, expressing some of the stereotypes of middle-class Americans who have never had to personally face the constant frustrations and barriers of poverty. Taylor sees the cruelty of his arguments—after all, she is living them—and takes a very personal revenge on him (210). Similar notions also appear when Annawake and Jax, in a telephone conversation, conclude that Cherokee myths inculcate the notion that one should "Do right by your people," while American myths suggest that the goal should be to "Do right by yourself" (88). The selflessness of the first and the selfishness of the second, when they are stated this way, are apparent. Kingsolver has often expressed deep distaste for the ideals associated with the Horatio Alger myth, and these reservations are clearly expressed in *Pigs in Heaven*.

Other themes, developed less insistently, are present in the novel. Recall the satire of certain notions of conventional femininity expressed through the characterization of Barbie. Consumerism, the desire for things whether or not they have any innate value or usefulness, is also satirized through this striking, comic, and yet appalling character. The importance of closeness to nature and the richness of simple lives spent in harmony with the natural world are also dramatized in this novel. Television, as a corrupting feature of contemporary culture, is attacked through Alice's dissatisfaction with her TV-loving husband, and it is significant that Cash finally proves his love for Alice and his worthiness to be her husband when he shoots his television set (242–44). The complexity and richness of thematic presentation, only sketched here, is one of the great strengths of *Pigs in Heaven*.

IMAGERY AND STYLE

Kingsolver's voice in *Pigs in Heaven*, although here used omnisciently rather than through the first-person narrative characteristic of her first two novels, remains strong and vivid. Her dialogue is rich with the speech patterns of her mostly uneducated but intelligent characters; their regional idioms and sometimes uncertain grammar are believably conveyed.

One storytelling device used sparingly but very importantly here is that of the illustrative story or parable. Two such tales, used to illuminate themes of the novel, are striking—one because of its explanation of the novel's unusual title, and the other because of its familiarity to the reader, although appearing in an unexpected context and form.

While the startling title of the book refers to a story explained early in the novel, it also picks up on some piggish images scattered throughout. Among these are Alice's awareness of the pigs on the farms around her in Kentucky and her memories of the pig farm in Mississippi where she grew up, whose odor remains vivid in her mind as typifying her youth. The actual reference of the title, however, is to a Cherokee myth which explains the origin of the constellation known in Western astronomy as the Pleiades or the Seven Sisters. Annawake tells Jax that in Cherokee lore there are only six stars in the cluster (a reminder of the way in which cultures may perceive even natural phenomena differently). Six little boys, she explains, were very naughty. They wouldn't stop playing ball and having fun, so finally their mothers put their balls into some soup and boiled it up and served it to them. The boys were angry, declaring that only pigs would eat that soup, so they run around yelling to the spirits that their mothers are mistreating them. The spirits hear them and answer their angry request, turning them into pigs which run faster and faster "till they were just a blur. Their little hooves left the ground and they rose up into the sky, and there they are" (88). To Annawake this myth means "Do right by your people," and she compares it to the Horatio Alger myth which Jax says typifies white American culture and means something like, "Do right by yourself" (88). Thus, the Cherokee myth expresses Native American values and is one summary of the conflict between individual and community that is at the heart of this novel.

The second story, told to Annawake by her uncle Ledger, is also identified as a Native American tale. He tells it in order to explain motherhood and love, and it concerns two clan mothers in conflict over a child, each claiming it and demanding that the Above Ones validate her claim. The Above Ones announce that they will send the snake Uk'ten to cut the child in half so that each mother may take part of it (330). Clearly, what Ledger has done is transpose the biblical tale of the wise Solomon (I Kings 3:16–27) into the mythic world of Cherokee belief. Annawake, recognizing the non-Native source of the parable, takes him to task and the subject is dropped, but the relevance of the story of the love of the mother who is willing to give up her child so that it not be harmed clearly has relevance to Taylor, who is now not certain that Turtle is best off with her. The use of this Hebrew-Cherokee story helps to explain the choices facing those who must decide what is to become of Turtle, and Kingsolver's use of the parable device to explain and intensify her meanings is effective.

Language throughout the novel is vivid and original. Some of this language recreates the speech of characters and helps to bring them alive, but the narrative voice also speaks with vigor and freshness. Mangling of words and phrases is one element of linguistic comedy. For example, the headline about Turtle's saving Lucky Buster after his fall over Hoover Dam in a small-town newspaper reads: "LUCKY BUSTER SAVED BY PERVERSERING TUSCON PAIR" (33), managing to pack two spelling errors into one brief phrase. One simply re-creates a frequent misspelling of a city name; the other includes a play on two very different words, "persevere" and "perverse." The first, "persevere" was intended, but Taylor reads literally and is puzzled and amused. Alice manages several comic but unintended plays on words, speaking of "artificial retrucidation" when she means "artificial resuscitation" (216) and referring to a "millionaire typhoon" instead of a "tycoon" (290). An example of particularly apt expression through the narrative voice is the description of the moment a light is switched on as "a thin slice of white cat, an antishadow" (58) walks by. Striking here is the reversal from black to white cat and from dark shadow to its imagined opposite, something like the antimatter which scientists say mirrors the matter of which our world is constructed.

A GENRE-BASED READING OF *PIGS IN HEAVEN*

Like all Kingsolver's work, *Pigs in Heaven* does not fit easily into any generic categories, except that of the political or issue-oriented novel. However, it does play with some characteristics of the genre most deeply imbedded in women's fiction, the romance. The usual romance moves toward a happy ending in which the female protagonist is united joyously with her lover, tying up all the loose strands of the narrative. One of the appeals of this genre is the comfortable awareness readers have that everything will work out well in the end. Thus, they are able to suffer with the protagonist, feeling her pain and rejection, knowing all along that the protagonist will finally be rewarded for her virtues.

Pigs in Heaven seems through much of its plot to point toward a happy ending, but the romantic union is not between the protagonist and her lover. The central plot is not a love story, and the primary element of the happy ending is, the compromise solution to Turtle's custody. In addition several possible romantic relationships are followed.

One of these liaisons is that between Taylor and Jax. In the usual romance, the female protagonist would be courted by the male figure with their union being ensured in the conclusion. Here, however, the two are together at the beginning of the novel and are separated without any intention of breaking up their relationship when Taylor flees because of the threat to her motherhood of Turtle. The threats to their love are twofold, Jax's unfaithfulness to Taylor and the danger of their growing apart because of the separation. The novel's end indicates that they will be reunited, as Jax has always wanted a more permanent connection and Taylor decides that she, too, hopes that something more durable, perhaps even marriage, may be established. She is ready for something lasting, no matter what happens about Turtle, she says. All of this indicates that her experiences have helped her to mature. At the end of *Pigs in Heaven*, just as at the end of *The Bean Trees*, Taylor is ready to return to her home in Tucson.

Another love affair is between Taylor's mother and the man who is the grandfather of Taylor's illegally adopted daughter. Many clues are given that the romantic union between Alice and Cash will be the first major step in resolving the conflict over custody of Turtle by indirectly returning Turtle to the care of her tribe in the person of Taylor, who now will have a closer claim to membership in the tribe. Because hints are dropped throughout the novel, readers are aware of Cash's connection with Turtle long before the characters have an idea of any such relationship.

One of the problems Kingsolver had to deal with in plotting this novel was the necessity of using coincidence. Alice happens to be part Cherokee. She happens to have been a close friend of her second cousin who now lives in Oklahoma and has become an enrolled member of the tribe. Turtle, the baby foisted on Taylor, Alice's daughter, happens to be the granddaughter of Cash, who happens to return to Oklahoma after the disappearance of his granddaughter but in time to begin a search for her, shortly before Alice travels to Oklahoma. Annawake Fourkiller happens to see Turtle and Taylor when they appear on the Oprah Winfrey talk show, immediately recognizing the child as a Cherokee. The love between Alice and Cash is not accidental, as Annawake and several confederates do some very effective matchmaking—Annawake because she perceives the possibility of a painless solution to the dilemma of what to do about Turtle. But the discovery by Alice and Cash of their connection through Turtle, even though it has long been expected by readers, seems contrived because it is built on the framework of a succession of coincidences. Such plotting, in which authors manipulate their characters to lead them to a happy ending which may not be justified by the plotting and characterization which precede it, is not uncommon in the romance. The requirements for a happy ending and a neat solution to all the problems set up in the novel overcome other considerations. This would seem to be what is happening in *Pigs in Heaven*.

However, the happy ending is not so easily achieved in this novel. It is not the protagonist but rather a subordinate character, Taylor's mother, who is involved in the courtship story. Annawake, who has been set up to be the villain from the novel's earliest sections, becomes a major manipulator as she encourages the romance between Alice and Cash. Taylor, who has most to gain by Annawake's actions, distrusts Annawake. Most significant, Cash and, especially, Alice resist being manipulated. Alice is so angry at the matchmaking, which she first believes was intended to make her sympathize with Cash and betray Taylor, that she breaks off her relationship with Cash. Her anger disrupts what had been a relatively smooth courtship and ironically briefly seems to risk the success of the compromise that Annawake had hoped to create.

When the happy ending occurs, it is despite the romantic motif, not because of it. A compromise is achieved through means of a romance, but it is worked out because it is in the best interests of both Turtle (to stay with Taylor, the only mother she has known) and the tribe (to have

Turtle visit her grandfather annually, so that she may be taught the culture of her people). Cash's very public marriage proposal to Alice and her implied consent seem almost afterthoughts. While Taylor will return with Turtle to Tucson and to Jax, now intending to marry him, Alice will remain in Oklahoma, to become an enrolled member of the tribe and marry Cash. Thus, in a pattern of a variation on the romance, *Pigs in Heaven* carries two unconventional romantic stories to happy conclusions.

6

The Poisonwood Bible
(1998)

Kingsolver's long-awaited novel set in late colonial and postcolonial Africa, making use of her memories of a childhood stay in that continent and of extensive reading, appeared in late 1998. This was three years after her last previous book-length publication, *High Tide in Tucson*, and five years after her last previous novel, *Pigs in Heaven*. A short story, called "My Father's Africa," which contains the germs of some of the ideas, characters, and incidents which were to be developed in *The Poisonwood Bible*, appeared in *McCall's* in August 1991, before the publication of *Pigs in Heaven*, and indicated that Kingsolver intended to begin research for the African novel while living on Tenerife. The short story introduces the novel's family, although it contains five, not the eventual four, daughters. Rae Ann is the name of the narrator, a daughter who may have been renamed Leah in the novel, evidenced by the fact that some of the materials in the short story reappear in that daughter's opening narrative. Rachel is present and shows clear indications of her later characterization, while Ruth May is mentioned as the smallest of the children. A daughter called Annalee is also present, although missing from the eventual novel, while Adah is a character in the novel but not the short story. The fifth daughter is unnamed. The basic situation of the family's arrival in Kilanga, as well as several anecdotes and images later appear in the novel. However, events move forward rapidly, giving a sketch of action which more fully and slowly developed in the novel.

The gap in time before the publication of *The Poisonwood Bible* was a change from the rapid succession of seven novels and other longer works which were issued in the eight years from 1988 through 1995, the beginnings of Kingsolver's career as a serious writer. It was known that she was working on a novel based on the experiences of an American missionary family in the Congo (Zaire). The lapse of time and a bibliography of twenty-nine items accompanying the novel indicate the seriousness of this endeavor and the amount of work it entailed. *The Poisonwood Bible* is Kingsolver's longest (at 546 pages) and most complex work to date. It covers a longer period of time, from 1959 to some time after 1986 (the last section is undated), unlike the earlier novels which occur in relatively short spans of time (*Animal Dreams*, for example, occurs essentially in one academic year, with a brief epilogue several years later). The narrative method is more complex than that of earlier novels, with the voices of five major characters being used. Thematically, this novel is also more complex; based on the actual history of what was the Belgian Congo and became Zaire, it combines that history with the history and experiences of the Price family. Africa itself becomes a force, almost a character, in the novel. In many ways, Kingsolver was attempting new things in this book, and it might be argued that despite the fine qualities and popular acceptance of her earlier works, it is with *The Poisonwood Bible* that she has reached true maturity as a novelist.

As is typical for Kingsolver, *The Poisonwood Bible* is immensely rich in both character and event, but is truly centered around thematic concerns. Like her other novels, this one began with a question, which in this case is concerned with issues of truth, justice, colonial occupation, and genocide ("Barbara Kingsolver," PBS *Signature* series). These are serious issues of the late twentieth-century postcolonial period, more often addressed by writers of the nations which were ruled by Western, developed nations than by writers of the colonial powers. In addressing them, Kingsolver is continuing in the vein she had established earlier, and importantly, broadening her concerns. The political radicalism so clearly developed in *The Poisonwood Bible* should come as no surprise to readers familiar with *Holding the Line*, the essays in *High Tide in Tucson*, or the short story, "Why I Am a Danger to the Public," which is the final piece in *Homeland*. She has addressed issues relating to the oppression of Native Americans within the United States and in Central America in her first three novels. In her poetry, *Another America/Otra America*, she has commented on the situation of Spanish-speaking Americans both within the United States and in Latin America. In her shorter fiction and occasionally in her essays, she has expanded her settings and themes. In the essays "Somebody's Baby" and "Paradise Lost," both included in *High Tide in Tucson*, she has commented on her life in the Canary Isles, where she exiled herself for a period of time in protest against the Gulf War. Her experiences as a child in St. Lucia inspired the short story "Jump-up Day," which appears in *Homeland*, and a trip to Africa taken as an adult is described in the essay entitled "The Vibrations of Djoogbe" in *High Tide in Tucson*. "Jump-up Day," with its use of cultural survival from Africa, and "The Vibrations of Djoogbe" are particularly significant in revealing Kingsolver's continuing interest in the life and people of Africa which were to receive their full development in *The Poisonwood Bible*.

SETTINGS

The first and most obvious observations about *The Poisonwood Bible* relate to its settings. Africa is the central subject, the setting, and, essentially, a character in the plot. The members of the Price family go to Africa on what is intended to be a twelve-month mission, are caught there by the coming of independence and ensuing political and military chaos, and find their lives totally changed by their African experience. Four of them remain in Africa, and only two return permanently to the United States. Africa, in various ways, overcomes them, destroys the family they had been, and changes them all in ways they never could have foreseen.

The novel opens from Sanderling Island, Georgia, as Orleanna Price, mother of the family, meditates retrospectively on her family's African past, long after her African experiences, and seeks to put them into some kind of perspective. Then the novel shifts to what is its most central setting, the village of Kilanga in the Congo, the place upon which the Reverend Nathan Price seeks to impose his will and his particular evangelical Baptist version of Christianity. This is also the place which defeats him and destroys his family, and it is the principal setting of the next several sections, which contain the novel's main action. Following these sections, as the novel moves more rapidly toward the present and the characters move from place to place, the settings are more varied but still mostly African, interspersed with a few chapters located in Georgia, from which the family had originally come and to which most of its members return—two of them permanently and one only for several brief visits. Most notable among the African settings outside of Kilanga are Johannesburg, Kinshasa, a convent, and a hotel.

The land and the people of what used to be called the "dark continent" are commanding presences in the novel, presented throughout the wanderings of the members of the Price family and, more powerfully, from their initial contacts with Africa. The opening passage, in which Orleanna describes a picnic on the river, sets a tone. Orleanna evokes the jungle, an environment completely foreign to her family, one which is at the same time lushly beautiful and ominously threatening. From this opening, which is at once broad in its introduction of the land and specific in its prelude to the family's story, the novel moves to a concentration on the specific with the Price daughters' stories told in their own words. The family's preparations for Africa have been ludicrous. They could bring only a small amount of luggage, and their preparations for housekeeping in a jungle village forced them to choose necessities, some of which turn out to be totally inappropriate. Not surprisingly the family members respond to their new surroundings, both land and people, in a variety of ways; the first response to their new place is bewilderment and misunderstanding. Only one, Leah, ever truly and completely overcomes her initial lack of comprehension.

From the beginning they misunderstand the land. Convinced that the soil which bears the lush jungle will respond to American agricultural methods, they attempt to plant a garden with familiar plants and tend it in their accustomed ways. A village woman scornfully tells them that their method will not work, but the Reverend Price persists, and the result is failure. To the Reverend Price, the nearby river is important for providing the water in which he will baptize all the converts which he expects to make. To the villagers, the river is a place of danger, and they cannot understand his compulsion to dip them in the river, the home of crocodiles and death. Their total alienness from each other makes the goal of Christianizing the village a lost cause.

Africa is also an oppressed world, a land which has had its rich mineral resources ripped from it and taken far away to benefit white Europeans. It is home to a people who have been brutally forced to destroy their resources while not even gaining good roads or other forms of modernization. Kingsolver skillfully conveys information about the history of the Congo's colonial past and the ruthless way in which its people were treated, including such inhumane punishments as the amputation of limbs for relatively minor infractions. That experience, already in the past as the novel gets under way, is vividly remembered by the people and explains their distrust of white faces. That they continue to have good reasons to hate outsiders with European origins is amply dramatized by the narrative. Eeben Axelroot, a pilot who ferries supplies into the jungles, and robs Africans and white people indiscriminately, serves as one example of the continuing exploitation of Africa by the West. The Prices' initial smug assumption of superiority is another.

Africa continues to be dominated politically. Leah learns of the U.S. Central Intelligence Agency's interference in the Congo's internal affairs. But on other levels, Africa triumphs. The land destroys Nathan's hopes, as the people remain stubbornly faithful to their history, culture, and ancestral roots. Nathan's garden fails, and his school is only partly successful as the students take from it only what they want, not what he wants to give them. Anatole Ngemba his translator, sees to it that the people know what Nathan is saying and what he is trying to achieve with them, so that they may decide for themselves if anything he brings is worth having. Nathan's struggle against the village's spiritual leader ends in total defeat and the death of a daughter. The Africans even turn the West's own methods against it. The notion of voting is foreign to the Africans, who are accustomed to respecting those with the experience of age and arriving at consensus. To them counting each person's vote as equal to that of every other person is ludicrous. However, the village leader destroys Nathan's mission by calling for a vote on whether they should adopt Nathan's God, and the voting is conducted under circumstances in which Nathan cannot refuse to allow the balloting. The voting goes against him. Africa's people triumph because of their maintaining their customs and beliefs and using, when convenient, the West's ideas for their own gain.

The people of the village are both scornful and kind to the Price family. The sense of community which they hold enables them both to laugh at the Price women who seek to make a home in an unyielding place, and to secretly assist them from time to time. Without some practical gifts from the women of the village, the survival of the Price family would have been dubious. As it is, they suffer from a variety of African torments. Ruth May, the youngest of the daughters, hates the bitter taste of her quinine pills and she secretly stops taking them; as a result, she contracts a serious case of malaria. A plague of ants, against which they have no defense, terrifies the family and they can only follow the villagers in escaping from this overwhelming force. Repeatedly African nature threatens to overwhelm the Prices.

Africa is a strong and ambiguous force. Kingsolver's depiction of the land is complicated—morally as well as in regard to its natural power. Like Joseph Conrad in *Heart of Darkness*, which is listed in her extensive bibliography, Kingsolver depicts in *The Poisonwood Bible* a continent which is seductive and which, while being corrupted by the colonial powers, may also corrupt the agents of those powers. Like Kurtz in *Heart of Darkness*, Nathan Price becomes sucked into the mystery and is ultimately destroyed by it. Unlike Conrad, however, Kingsolver does not persuade the reader that the evil of her version of Kurtz represents an inevitable outcome. Leah's experience of staying in Africa and becoming a member of the native community is the most obvious example of other, more positive possibilities.

STRUCTURE AND PLOT DEVELOPMENT

The plot of *The Poisonwood Bible* interlaces the stories of six members of the Price family with the story of the newly independent country of the Congo (later Zaire). The basic structure of the novel is made up of seven "books," the first six named for a book of the Bible or a passage of the Apocrypha (Old Testament books not considered part of the Hebrew or Protestant canon; they are not included in the King James Bible). Each of these sections, except the sixth, opens with a chapter narrated some time after the family's African experiences by Orleanna Price, the mother of the family, and each contains a succession of chapters from the points of view of the family's four daughters. The first five books are dated. The first four take place during times of particular significance both to the family and to the history of the Congo. The fifth book differs by dating each separate narrative and covering a span of fifteen years. The sixth book lacks an introductory passage by Orleanna and contains only one chapter from each of the daughters, bringing the story nearer to the present. Finally, the last book, serving as a brief epilogue only six and a half pages long, returns to some of the imagery of Orleanna's opening passage at the beginning of the first book. It differs from all the other books in that its title is not biblical; rather it comes from imagery internal to the novel. It also lacks the biblical epigraphs which accompany all of the other books. What Kingsolver has done structurally is to base much of her presentation on biblical ideas—quite suitably, given the missionary calling of the head of the family—and to connect those biblical ideas to the chronology of her story and the history of the nation which serves as her major setting.

Kingsolver's plot may be summarized in part through the subtitles given to the first five sections. The first book, appropriately entitled "Genesis" (beginning) after the opening book of the Bible, is set in the last months of colonial rule over the Congo and depicts the arrival and first acclimating difficulties of the Price family. It has the subtitle, "The Things We Carried," referring to their carefully selected but inappropriate supplies. It also refers to the emotional, psychological, intellectual, and religious "baggage" which they brought with them, intangible things that ill prepared them to survive and prosper in utterly alien surroundings.

The second book is entitled "The Revelation," echoing the title of the final book of the Christian Bible. Dated June 30, 1960—when the Congo achieved independence—it is subtitled, "The Things We Learned." The mission in Kilanga continues and the family become somewhat better able to cope with the new world which is being "revealed" to them. The next book, called "The Judges" after the biblical book of Judges, is dated September 1960, only a few months later, indicating the relatively slow pace of these early sections. It is subtitled, "The Things We Didn't Know," emphasizing the failure of the family to truly become a part of their surroundings.

For book four, a title from the Apocrypha is used, "Bel and the Serpent." The date is January 17, 1961, and the subtitle is "What We Lost." The most obvious loss to the family is the death of Ruth May, the youngest daughter, and her death is connected with the failure of Nathan's mission—his overt defeat by Africa—and with the breakup of the family, for after Ruth May's death, Orleanna takes her remaining children and leaves. Book five, "Exodus" (going out), named for the second biblical book in which the Hebrews fled Egypt and escaped from their period of slavery, is subtitled "What We Carried Out" and is paired and contrasted with the first book, "Genesis." Similar to the first book, book five's subtitle refers both to the few physical objects they took with them and to the emotional wounds and psychological lessons which had become a part of them after their experiences in Kilanga. This book bears no single date, but follows the three remaining daughters as they seek to make lives for themselves after Kilanga, lives which differ radically for each of the three. Book six, entitled "Song of the Three Children," also from the Apocrypha, is relatively brief and contains only one chapter for each daughter. With varying degrees of insight, each narrator attempts to sort it all out, to explain to herself what it all meant both for herself and for her sisters. Thus, several views of each daughter, her own and her sisters' assumptions, are included. Book seven, "The Eyes in the Trees," pulls back, giving a broader view of the whole experience, a view which is both symbolic and mystical, evoking the understanding of Ruth May—now the outside observer who is Africa.

NARRATIVE METHOD AND CHARACTER DEVELOPMENT

The Poisonwood Bible is told entirely in first-person narrative, but the voices shift from chapter to chapter. The principal narrators are the women of the Price family: the mother, Orleanna, and the four daughters, Rachel, Leah, Adah, and Ruth May. Orleanna, remembering events much later from her home on Sanderling Island, Georgia, tries to give her experiences perspective and meaning in her relatively brief narratives which open each of the first five books. The daughters, in various orders, carry the weight of actually relating the story, each telling in her own voice about events in which she was involved and commenting on what they meant to her. Additionally each daughter makes evaluations of her own actions and those of her sisters and parents as well. This procedure is followed until book six: Orleanna's voice is missing but each surviving daughter sums up where she is and what has brought her to that place in her life. By this point the narration of events has largely ceased and what remains is introspection. Finally, in the last book, all the familiar narrative voices are gone; the brief narrative of this almost mystical voice ties things together and broadens both the meanings and the emotional impact of the novel. This voice expresses the perspective of the dead daughter who is united with the African soil, of the "eyes in the trees" which have seen all that has occurred and have been unchanged by the often frantic and misguided actions of the characters in the novel—the perspective of Africa.

This narrative approach developed out of the method Kingsolver had practiced in earlier novels, first in the opening chapters of *The Bean Trees* and then more notably in *Animal Dreams*. In both of those works, Kingsolver makes use of shifting points of view to tell parts of her story from several different perspectives; however, one primary narrative voice— Taylor Greer in *The Bean Trees* and Codi Noline in *Animal Dreams*—prevails. In *The Poisonwood Bible*, five characters speak, and of them, the three daughters who live to adulthood are given independent lives to recount and significant portions of the novel in which to tell their stories.

It is true, however, that Leah, the daughter who comes to best understand and sympathize with Africa and the Africans, is the most sympathetic character and thus has emotional primacy in the recounting of
the daughters' adventures.

The list of the novel's principal narrators is essentially the same as the
list of major characters, with two important exceptions. Omitted is the
voice of Nathan Price, the father of this very patriarchal family. It is
significant that he never speaks for himself but is seen only through the
eyes of his wife and daughters. Marlow, Joseph Conrad's narrator in
Heart of Darkness, attempts to understand the enigmatic Kurtz, but must
remain entirely outside of the other man's perspective and understanding of Africa. Similarly, Orleanna and her daughters cannot enter into
the mind of their fanatical husband and father, although they are with
him from the beginning and observe his attempts to force his will upon
Africa. As Marlow is separated from Kurtz, so too the women are separated from Nathan during the time of his greatest change by Africa and
are finally left with a mystery and an enigma. His point of view from
the beginning is extreme and incomprehensible to the Africans whom he
lives among and whom he intends to change; it is appropriate that his
words are reported by others and thus filtered through their understand-
ings. Kingsolver does provide some explanation for his fanaticism in his
experience as a Japanese prisoner during World War II. This character
development, given from his wife's point of view and partly intended
to explain the origins of their marriage, does help to humanize him to a
degree for the reader. Nevertheless he remains a stranger to his wife and
daughters.

The other significant character who does not participate in the narration is Anatole Ngemba, the African who becomes Leah's husband and
who represents the progressive and revolutionary spirit of educated Africans. His story can be pieced together through Leah's narrative, and
his perspective on the events becomes clear, but like Nathan, he does
not speak for himself. Appropriately, the narrative voices of this novel
about the women in an American family are restricted almost entirely to
those women. Just as in *Holding the Line* where Kingsolver's subject is
the women involved in the Phelps Dodge strike and the story is limited
to their experiences, the novel's focus on the Price women as the true
center of the family, despite its patriarchal nature, dictates the bounda-
ries of the narrative voices.

The voices of the Price daughters are artfully conveyed in language
which is always appropriate to each daughter and which changes

through time as they grow and change. The naiveté with which all four daughters tell of their preparations for the journey to Africa and describe their early impressions communicates both their ignorance about their new home and their youth and inexperience. As they gradually learn more about Africa and Africans and as they grow older, their language changes. Additionally, they are clearly differentiated from each other; a reader could never confuse the voice of Rachel, which is shallow, peppered with malapropisms, and illustrates her self-centeredness and concern for material possessions, with that of Adah, which is unexpectedly playful, contains frequent allusions to the poetry of Emily Dickinson, and reveals her penchant for mirror-writing. Leah's greater depth, though she is younger than Rachel, is evident from the beginning in her more obvious efforts to understand what she sees. Finally, Ruth May's childish prattle is also clearly and effectively delineated. In each case, the language of the narrative voice is an important part of the characterization.

As the opening narrative voice, Orleanna Price, wife of Nathan Price and mother of his four daughters, sets the initial tone of the novel. She begins by describing the picnic in Africa which will be referred back to in the final book, thereby completing the novel's frame. She is a relatively subordinate character, at least in comparison to her daughters, but her characterization is nevertheless full and believable. She is a sensitive and loving mother and an abused wife who stays with her husband because she believes that is the right thing to do and also because she does not know what else to do. Her marriage becomes a nightmare in Kilanga, for housekeeping in the terms in which she understands it is impossible there. She is dependent in part on the kindness of some of the village women, and her husband has no understanding of or sympathy with the difficulties she faces every day in trying to care for her children. Her attempts to feed the girls, Ruth May's malaria, the horrible plague of ants which overruns the village and kills everything in its path—these are only a few of the trials which Orleanna faces and survives. One telling moment comes early in their stay in Kilanga when an angry Nathan smashes a plate which Orleanna treasured since it was one of the few reminders of home which she had managed to bring with her. She quietly accepts its loss, agreeing with her tyrannical husband that she was "too fond of that plate" (134) and almost cowering before him.

In the familiar pattern of abused women, she remains with him, despite his mistreatment and despite her doubts, until the climactic moment in which her youngest daughter dies, a victim of Africa. When that occurs, she finally rebels and acts decisively. Nathan seems concerned only that Ruth May was not yet baptized, but Orleanna ignores him, methodically cleaning and preparing her child's body for burial and giving away many of her own possessions to women of the village. There is a grotesque funeral in which Nathan baptizes the children of the village, "imploring the living progeny of Kilanga to walk forward into the light" (375), words which are echoed in the novel's last line. Orleanna finally gathers together her living children and they walk out of the jungle, leaving Nathan behind. These events are described at the end of book four, entitled "Bel and the Serpent," and the beginning of book five, "Exodus." A serpant bite has killed Ruth May, but this has led to the escape of the remaining women of the family, with the new strength for Orleanna: a formerly abused wife rescuing her living children.

Orleanna returns to Georgia and makes a new life for herself, although this is mostly not seen, but rather referred to in retrospect and kept off stage. Her last narration, the introduction to book five, carries her into the pain of her flight and picks up some of the imagery of her opening lines in book one, thereby also pointing forward to the novel's final section. Although her later life is referred to from time to time in the narratives of her daughters, her real part in the action of the novel is now complete.

When the four Price daughters are introduced, at the time of their removal to Africa, they are children, the oldest, Rachel, being fifteen years old and the others ranging downward. Rachel is the least changed of the four by her African experience. She is shallow and self-centered at the beginning, and she remains so until the end. Her narrative voice is characterized by intense concentration on her appearance, on the way she appears to others, and on her own comfort. Clothing, her mirror, and cosmetic items are of great importance to Rachel. She is amusingly prone to use big words which she does not understand, and as a result, her narratives are peppered with various sorts of linguistic errors, mainly malapropisms—words incorrectly used in place of other similar sounding words—and with misuse of grammatical forms. A few examples chosen at random will illustrate. The young Rachel speaks of one of her sisters "fixing to executrate [execute]" a "swoon" (22). The ritual scarring on Anatole's face, she says, "gave him a mysterious air, like a putative [fugitive] from the law" (125). The missionaries who had preceded the Price family to Kilanga were "Episcopotamians" [Episcopalians] (159). Leah quotes her as referring to a "child-progeny [prodigy] sister" (242). Rachel once comments that she prefers "to remain anomalous [anonymous]" (271). When she makes literary allusions, they are often mangled, as when she mentions "Gulliver among the Lepidopterans" [Lilliputians] (269). Sometimes her misstatements make a comic sense of their own, as with "anomalous" and "Lepidopterans," for example. Her narrative is full of slang and clichés in early years, containing many references to U.S. advertising slogans as well, although the last gradually decrease as Rachel's distance in time from her American experience lengthens. Years later, her grammar and vocabulary have improved somewhat, but her narration is just as breezy and centered around her own precious self as it had been earlier. Her invincible ignorance is as complete as ever, as when she offhandedly asks if Karl Marx is "still in charge of Russia" (478) and accepts the public statements of Ronald Reagan and Henry Kissinger as absolute truth even when, as Leah points out, she should know the facts of African history which make their comments into nonsense (478).

Throughout the novel, Rachel is the silly one of the daughters, but she is also the one who always lands on her feet. Her selfishness enables her to keep her eye on what will be best for her, and she has few, if any, scruples about the behavior she uses to forward her own welfare. A platinum blonde, she is the most strikingly foreign-looking member of the family, and her appearance—of which she is inordinately proud— becomes both a danger and her salvation. When a polygamous tribal chieftain decides he wants her as his second wife, a fate far worse than death to Rachel, she immediately becomes formally engaged to Eeben Axelroot, the unscrupulous pilot. After the Price women escape from Kilanga, Rachel becomes his mistress, calling herself Rachel Price Axelroot and living as his wife although they are never married. Later, she uses two other men to improve her situation, although those two liaisons are mentioned only in passing. She once refers to herself as "Rachel Axelroot DePree Fairley" (460), remarkably including several names to which she has no legal right and omitting her birth surname.

She moves from man to man, until finally, as she puts it, she "got lucky in love" with a man who "had the decency to die and leave me the Equatorial" (461), the hotel in Brazzaville which she runs happily. Finally independent, able to support herself comfortably, and the most important person in her particular place, she decides that she no longer needs men. She has at least matured to the point of being a more nearly autonomous individual who controls her own situation and life. But she is still the same selfish person she has always been, still concerned primarily about herself, still happily ignorant of the world surrounding her, and still completely unconcerned about the welfare of others. Because of her frank and unconcealed selfishness and her breezy narration, she is the flattest and least believable of the novel's significant characters, but she also frequently serves as welcome comic relief. She represents one extreme of ex-patriate women who not only resist assimilation into their second world but remain almost totally untouched by it. Rachel, it must be admitted, is not completely unaffected by her African experience, however, for she ultimately becomes a displaced person, always a foreigner where she lives and a foreigner to her native land, unable to return there. Of the surviving Price women, she is the most stubbornly American and, ironically, the only one never to return to the United States.

Next in age to Rachel are twins, Leah and Adah, who are totally different from each other beginning in childhood and continuing throughout the paths their lives take. Adah, the second born, was the victim of hemiplegia, a birth defect which left half of her brain undeveloped. As a result, one side of her body is poorly coordinated, and she walks with a serious limp. Her linguistic abilities are also affected, both for good and ill. She is mute, but she has the gift of a certain kind of wordplay, being able to read both from left to right and from right to left. Her early narratives are filled with palindromes—phrases which read the same backwards and forwards—and sometimes require that the reader take the time to transpose nonsense phrases into conventional English. This interest in language and a particular from of wordplay characterizes Adah's voice just as the grammatical and vocabulary errors characterize Rachel's.

Adah's interest in language for its own sake extends to her interest in and love of poetry. She refers to several poets, but the poems of Emily Dickinson are particularly crucial. Dickinson is an interesting choice. As a woman poet who became a recluse and spoke through her poetry to a world from which she felt alienated, her appeal to Adah seems obvious. Like Dickinson, Adah is a keen observer but not a participant; like Dickinson, she is sensitive to the feelings of others. Furthermore, like Dickinson, she is the daughter of an autocratic, extremely patriarchal father and a weak mother, neither of whom seems to understand her or rightly value her.

Life changes dramatically for Adah after the escape from Kilanga. She and her mother return to the United States. Adah's condition is finally properly diagnosed and she can be helped to become "normal." After treatment and therapy, she is able to walk without a limp, and she decides to speak. The intelligence which has characterized her narrations enables her to acquire a formal education and even to complete medical school. She becomes a doctor, specializing in research of tropical diseases. But the gains are accompanied by losses: her special linguistic abilities are gone, she now speaks, but the poetry is no more. She revisits Africa, but unlike Rachel and Leah, she is at home in the United States, where she and her mother attempt to understand what has happened to them all in Africa.

Adah's twin, Leah, is the most memorable of the Price women. If any one character serves as protagonist, it is Leah. She is the most changed and she becomes the wisest and most mature of the daughters. Verlyn Klinkenborg calls her the "conscience of this striking novel" (7). She is the one who becomes truly a part of African society. Her transformation is shown gradually. At the beginning, she is just as confused and frightened as the others by Kilanga. She, like them, compares what she sees there with what she had been accustomed to, considering African ways strange and different. She believes her father to be immensely wise. But she soon forms a friendship with Anatole, the translator and schoolteacher, and this relationship is crucial for her. He helps her see that American ways are not necessarily the only ways, that there may be several different and valid ways of looking at things. His openness and dedication to truth and to the welfare of his people teach her a great deal. At the same time, she gradually comes to see her father's flaws and loses her originally unquestioning faith in his brand of Christianity.

Leah's relationship with Anatole ripens into love and, eventually, after a long and trying time when Anatole is imprisoned for his political beliefs and she waits for him in a Roman Catholic convent, they are married. Their lives are then dedicated to working for the betterment of Zaire, the name by which the Congo was known during this period. Their visits to the United States are for the very practical purpose of gaining education to increase their usefulness to their people. Although Leah's physical appearance makes her always something of an anomaly in Africa, she dresses like African women, lives like them, and eventually feels herself an African, not an American. A revolutionary and Marxist like her husband, she is part of Africa.

The youngest of the Price children, Ruth May, does not live to maturity and her narrative voice remains childish. Her youthful babbling is characterized by extreme naiveté and by uncritically echoing the opinions of her parents. Her misunderstandings are often both pointed and comic, as when she describes, without full comprehension, some of the cruelties of segregation in the United States, approvingly referring to "the man in church" who says that "they" are different from white people and "needs ought to keep to their own," adding confusedly that "Jimmy Crow says that, and he makes the laws" (20). Her early sections, therefore, because they echo so straightforwardly the beliefs, both social and religious, that she has taken from her parents and the segregated society from which she has come, give good insights into who the Price family are and the culture they are bringing with them to the Congo.

Ruth May's early characterization is as a rather charming child, one who prattles on about things she doesn't really understand and thus transmits to the reader more information than she intends. She seems doomed from the beginning, refusing to take her quinine pills because they taste bad and sticking them on the wall by her bed, where they are later discovered after she has contracted a serious case of the malaria they were intended to prevent. She survives the malaria, however, only to die in a strange combination of events which a number of forces and people, on both national and village levels, combine to bring about. As Leah observes, "You can't just point to the one most terrible thing and wonder why it happened. . . . Each bad thing causes something worse" (327). At the achievement of independence for the Congo, Patrice Lumumba becomes president and then is captured by enemies and killed. The villagers using the device of voting—alien to them—decide that Jesus Christ will not be accepted "in the office of personal God, Kilanga village" (330). In general, the feelings of the villagers, led by their local chieftain who has many reasons to resent and hate Nathan Price, are running high, and the chieftain cleverly works to make their situation even more untenable. In a horrible combination of miscalculation on his part and the children being where they should not have been, Ruth May is killed by a snake bite, an event briefly seen from the perspective of each of her sisters. This event is pivotal for the girls' mother, who immediately takes her surviving daughters and flees from Kilanga, breaking up the family forever.

Ruth May has been the unwitting instrument of the destruction of her family, according to Klinkenborg, "the catalyst that splits the family apart" (7). In so doing, she is the first to be completely and irrevocably changed by Africa. The African snake, put in place by an African chieftain trying to maintain his power over his people and force out an alien intruder, is the direct cause of her death, but it is in truth both the land and the people of Africa who kill her. In death, she becomes one with the land, for she is buried there. Later when her sisters try to return to her grave, it has disappeared into the jungle, making her even more indissolubly a part of the place. Her eyes become the "eyes in the trees" which see all and eventually create the overview which closes and gives final meaning to the novel.

Ruth May is in some senses an odd choice for the mystical vessel which unites with Africa and reveals its victory. In other ways, however, this use of her seems utterly appropriate. As the youngest child and the least formed, she is most open to achieving a nonverbal, nonintellectual union with the land. Her victimization is the most pathetic which could have been depicted because of her very youth and childishness. The accidental quality of her death is underlined by the fact that she is bitten while childishly tagging along after her elders.

All of this gives Ruth May a very different quality than the other members of her family. She, like them, is portrayed as a very realistic and believable character. But the others all remain realistic, with the partial exception of Nathan in the later portions of the novel when he, by his very absence, takes on mythic qualities. She becomes as much symbol as real, and this symbolic use is carefully prepared. Her eyes are stressed, foreshadowing the motif of the "eyes in the trees," and her death is also presaged by her unintentionally inflicting malaria on herself by refusing quinine pills. She thus becomes the single character in the novel whose dual functions are necessitated by the book's structure and whose position in that structure is more importantly symbolic than it is realistic.

Two additional characters, different because they are males and because they do not participate in the narration of the novel, must also be briefly examined. They are Nathan Price and Anatole Ngemba, two men as different from each other as possible. Nathan is a white man, a fanatic Christian, determined to impress conservative Baptist Christianity on a people and a land which he does not understand. He is the head of a very patriarchal family and allows no opposition to his beliefs and actions. Adah ironically refers to him as "Our Father," echoing the opening words of the Lord's Prayer and commenting on his godlike position in his family. He is ultimately destroyed by his inability to comprehend other ways of living or thinking. Anatole is an African, probably more highly educated than Nathan, not a very religious man but one who dedicates himself to ensuring his people have the knowledge they need in order to make important decisions. He is as dedicated to the cause of his people—political and economic justice—as Nathan is dedicated to his God. He is to some degree like Nathan—an outsider who comes from a different (tribal) background than that of the people of Kilanga. But unlike Nathan, Anatole can see his cause clearly and objectively. Both men desire what they believe is best for the people of Kilanga, and both men are devoted to ideas which come from outside: Nathan to Christianity, and Anatole to socialism and Western ideas of education. But Nathan insists that the old ways of the people must be given up; the baptism in the river symbolizes their adoption of Christianity and discard of what Nathan considers pagan ways. Anatole, on the other hand, understands the values of the village system and is able to work with people to help them move forward and develop their own potential.

The very different paths their lives take after the Congo gains political independence and the Price women leave Kilanga result from their own beliefs and characters. The fanatic Nathan, now alone, penetrates deeper into the jungle, apparently sinking into madness, as he journeys farther and farther into his own "heart of darkness." His self-imposed exile cuts him off completely from his family and from any others like himself. In later years, he is known to his family only from snippets of news or gossip that come to them from deep within the jungle. Anatole, on the other hand, is imprisoned for his beliefs, but after release is united with Leah. While Nathan goes ever more into isolation, Anatole becomes part of a new and loving family, with a devoted wife—who is also a true helpmate—and four sons. He continues to teach and work for his people, and eventually he and Leah settle in Angola, where they find work that both fulfills them and helps their people. Nathan's and Anatole's lives are as different as their belief systems and their characters. Nathan's dreams open the novel, as he takes his family on a well-intentioned, if ill-conceived, mission to the Congo; Anatole's hopes are at the heart of the novel's conclusion. Nathan's life looks toward the colonial past, while Anatole's looks toward a more hopeful future.

THEMATIC DEVELOPMENT

Like Kingsolver's preceding three novels, *The Poisonwood Bible* is developed around strong themes. For this book, the thematic concerns which have engaged her attention are particularly ambitious: questions about truth, justice, colonialism, and genocide. These are characteristic issues for the Third World in the period after World War II; and her choice of the Congo where she, like the Price girls, had lived as a girl (though only briefly), seems obvious. In the twentieth century the Congo has emerged from a period of colonial rule by Belgium, rule which even in the context of the suffering of many peoples around the world in the last hundred years was particularly horrendous. The novel begins in the last days, literally, of the colonial rule, and the period of colonialism itself is developed mostly through allusions to the past. These allusions are enough to indicate the brutality with which the Congolese were treated by their European masters and the greed with which the land's rich resources were exploited. Following the independence that occurs within months of the Price family's arrival, colonial intervention does not cease, although it is expressed differently. The descent of the land into chaos parallels the Prices' complex and disillusioning initiation to African nature and people. In a telling image, the Congolese people are likened to the ants which have briefly overrun the village. During the family's flight from the ants—who, like the insects of a biblical plague, are devouring everything in their path—Leah, in anger, says God hates them. Anatole tells her not to blame God, that the ants, like the Congolese people, are just doing what they have to. "When they are pushed down long enough they will rise up. If they bite you, they are trying to fix things in the only way they know" (308). This interpretation presents the people as being an irresistible force, overwhelming in their numbers, and certain to carry all before them. They have the justification of necessity.

The mistreatment of Africa and Africans comes from many different sources. Brutality and cruelty are depicted as belonging not to the former Belgian colonial masters only, nor to the distant American politicians responsible for placing in power and continuing a corrupt political system. The custom of female circumcision, misunderstood and called "circus mission" by childish Ruth May (271), is briefly referred to. The ants are frighteningly unbiased; they will kill any living thing in their paths, leaving only the bones of the chickens and other village animals who were not able to escape. The Congolese participate in the exploitation of their own people. Although the American CIA and other outside influences may support the reactionary internal forces, the Congolese people cooperate with them to kill President Lumumba and, in the view of Anatole, to destroy the greatest opportunity for immediate justice and prosperity which the Congo had. The succeeding government, a government ostensibly by Congolese, is propped up by Western powers.

The political themes, concerning genocide and colonialism, are predominant and are examined with the same complexity and, often, subtlety as in her earlier novels. Equally compelling in *The Poisonwood Bible* are the family themes. The Price family is depicted as an extremely patriarchal one, with Nathan as its complete head commanding his wife and daughters, with their acquiescence, at his will. Orleanna, it is revealed, is an abused wife, and the psychological abuse worked on the daughters is evident. They have all accepted Nathan's absolute authority over them, and it is only gradually, as their experiences of a world which he cannot bend to his will teach them that he is fallible, that they begin to doubt him. This realization is made evident as the girls, especially Leah, gradually begin developing doubts of the God he preaches. His fanaticism and the absolute control which it necessitates are broken, completely and finally, when the village has the audacity to outvote his mission. (It should be noted that Nathan's loss of patriarchal control over his family parallels the ending of overt colonial rule over the Congo.) His loss of power is paired with his losses of a daughter to death and the rest of his family by flight. His control, so absolute, could not bend but could be only broken and destroyed. A contrasting model is found in the marriage of Leah and Anatole, with its example of cooperation between husband and wife, of loving concern for each other, of working together to accomplish the betterment of their people.

Another major, and related, theme developed in *The Poisonwood Bible* is that of clashing cultures and the difficulties people have in understanding others with differing basic assumptions about the world. Nathan Price is certain when he goes to Africa that he will quickly be able to teach the Africans how to lead civilized lives and to convert them to Christianity, to be symbolized by their baptism in the nearby river. It is soon brought home to him that the river is not a place for people to enter, even for ritual purposes. Instead, crocodile-infested, it is a place of death. Furthermore, the very notion of baptism is meaningless to the people. Villagers laugh at the way the Prices set up their first garden. Even Rachel, shallow though she is, quickly realizes that things are not at all what they had anticipated, observing that they had expected to be "calling the shots here, but it doesn't look to me like we're in charge of a thing, not even our own selves" (22). On every level—religious, agricultural, housekeeping, even simple survival—the villagers know how to live, despite the surroundings that are difficult and dangerous; but the Prices are outsiders who had foolishly attempted to bring their culture with them in the form of the Bible and Betty Crocker cake mixes, to name only two artifacts of importance to them. Gradually and resentfully, they must adapt, learning and accepting kindnesses from the villagers. It is to no avail: the village rejects them as still alien and the women flee. Alone, Nathan goes deeper into the jungle, by then his sanity in doubt. Driven by his obsession, he is nonetheless conquered by Africa. Many scenes illustrate the differences between Americans and Africans and their inability to understand each others' ways of life.

One of the strengths of Kingsolver's novels is that even the minor scenes illustrate, and thereby reinforce, the theme. Many episodes of lesser importance serve to illustrate the differences between Americans and Africans and their inability to understand the other's way of life. For example, there is a poignant yet minor moment when Leah, amazed by the power of the jungle, tries to describe to Anatole the size of American crop fields and the machinery used to cultivate them. He is simply unable to comprehend.

The novel is rich in other themes; notable among them are the ecological concerns, depicted partly in descriptions of the jungle, partly in the Prices' difficulty in learning the different gardening and farming methods. Other themes relate to family life: the abuse visited on the Price women within their patriarchal family structure, sibling relationships, and mother-daughter relationships, to name a few.

LANGUAGE AND SYMBOLISM

Kingsolver's uses of and interest in language are as important in *The Poisonwood Bible* as in her earlier fiction. The skill with which narrative voices are distinguished from each other and the manner in which they change as the Price daughters grow and mature have already been discussed. Also of interest is the use made in Adah's early narratives of several specific forms of wordplay and literary allusiveness. Recall her facility with palindromes. They are particularly frequent in early narratives, and they often bear important relevance to the action or themes being developed. The word "live" and its backward version "evil" appear often. One striking example comes in the private words to the familiar hymn, "Amazing Grace," which Adah sings:

> *Evil, all . . . its sin . . . is still . . . alive!*
> *Do go . . . Tata . . . to God!*
> *Sugar don't. . . . No, drag us*
> *drawn onward,*
> *A, he rose . . . ye eyesore, ha!* (72–73; ellipses and italics are
>   Kingsolver's)

The ambiguous linking of life and evil, of God, of resurrection ("rose") and ugliness ("eyesore"), and the encouragement of "Tata" (a polite title for men) are Adah's mute comment on her father's attempts to convert the villagers.

In addition to using this sort of wordplay, Adah is a lover of poetry. Allusions to the poems of Emily Dickinson are particularly prominent, and snippets from Dickinson's verse are generally used to comment appropriately on what Adah observes. For example, poignantly, she uses Dickinson's famous "Because I could not stop for death" in describing Ruth May's quick but painful death by snakebite, loosely but meaningfully paraphrasing, "and oh how dear we are to ourselves when it comes, it comes, that long, long shadow in the grass" (365).

The most important linguistic motif, however, relates to the use of the Bible, which is connected to the structure of the novel as well. Many names bear biblical significance. (A notable exception is the family's surname, which is secular but nevertheless symbolic. "Price" refers to the price they all must pay for the arrogance with which they—particularly Nathan—approach the Congo.) The Price family comes from Bethlehem, Georgia, a place named for the birthplace of Jesus Christ, whom they intend to reveal to the Congolese. The two eldest daughters, Rachel and Leah, bear the biblical names of two sisters who are both married to the same man. The parrot who was left in the mission by their predecessor and becomes a significant feature of early narratives is named for the long-lived Methuselah of the Bible. His use of phrases in both English and Kikongo so irritates Nathan that he finally frees the parrot. But Methuselah is accustomed to his imprisonment and he does not go far; he turns up frequently around the village through long portions of the story. He illustrates the way in which the security of prisons can become more important than the risks of freedom, an appropriate reminder in this story of colonialism. Adah, herself a cripple with a fellow feeling for him, points out that Methuselah is not prepared for freedom, that his caged years had atrophied his wings so that he cannot fly well (137). Finally he is killed by a civet cat, and it is Adah who finds him on the Congolese Independence Day. As she does so often, she quotes a poem by Emily Dickinson, " 'Hope' is the thing with feathers," as she grieves for him. Yet she can also rejoice, likening his death—his release from being "caged away from flight and truth" into the freedom which for him could be only death—to the new independence and freedom of the Congo (185–86).

The title of the novel is significant on several levels, most notably for the way in which it combines biblical (and thus Western) and African motifs. The novel itself is a kind of bible, a spiritual book telling stories with deep spiritual meanings. But it is a bible based in Africa, on African land and peoples, and the use of the poisonwood tree as a descriptor in its title is very important. The Kikongo language is a complex one with different meanings often attached to what seems to be the same word to the outsider's ear. The word written "bangala" refers to the poisonwood tree, a tree so deadly that when it burns, its smoke can kill. To those who do not understand the jungle and its culture, it is an appropriate symbol for the cruelty of Africa. Africans recognize the tree and its wood instantly and are able to avoid its danger, while outsiders are in danger of stoking fireplaces with the sticks of the deadly wood, as Orleanna does once. Fortunately, a village woman sees the danger (93).

But "bangala"—written the same but with a sight variation in pronunciation—also means something very precious. Nathan preaches with the phrase, "Tata Jesus is bangala" (276), ironically mispronouncing the final word so that instead of his intended meaning he is saying that Jesus is poisonwood, inspiring Adah, now disillusioned with her father's faith, to call it the "gospel of poisonwood" (276). To the people, what Nathan actually says is truth, for they feel no need for the alien—and to them meaningless—religion; to Nathan himself what he actually says is blasphemous. Adding to the irony is Nathan's insistence on a literal interpretation of his Bible, which contrasts with the gentler version that had been preached by his predecessor. That man had, in vain, pointed out that some of the native songs, such as a "hymn to the rainfall on the seed yams," are similar to Christian parables (in this case, the parable of the mustard seed). But his method requires him to "change a few words" (247), an impossible liberty to Nathan. Nathan, whose inadvertent misuse through ignorance of the native language is truly blasphemous, refuses to recognize the wisdom of his predecessor's acceptance of that which is good in the spirituality of the people. Nathan's Bible, as preached in Africa, is indeed a voice of poison, the expression of a religion which like political and economic colonialism takes no heed of the people themselves, their needs and gifts.

Kingsolver has chosen to mine the Bible for structural elements of her book. As previously discussed, the books of *The Poisonwood Bible* take their titles and epigraphs from biblical books or apocryphal passages, and these are significant to the action and themes she is developing. The opening book is entitled "Genesis," named for the opening book of the Bible. Its epigraph comes from Genesis 1:28, an admonition from God to

His newly created human beings to multiply and "have dominion . . . over every living thing." This faith in the power of humanity over nature, characteristic in Kingsolver's view of Western thought, is at the heart of the arrogance with which Nathan approaches Africa and the Africans as his mission begins. The subtitle, "The Things We Carried," in this context points out that they come encumbered with useless objects and with a faith which is not natural to this land. Theirs is therefore a beginning in pride, one which is doomed to failure because it is centered on itself, not on the land or people to which it has come.

The second book takes its title from the other end of the Bible, the book of Revelation, a much-discussed and debated piece full of symbols which are often believed to predict what will happen in the final times. It is Christ's revelation to his faithful of what is to come, and the epigraph suggests the visionary quality of the biblical book. It is taken from Revelation 13:1 and 9, a passage in which the narrator speaks of seeing a beast rise from the sea and calls on those who can to hear. Kingsolver adds a definite article, calling this section of her novel, "The Revelation," which makes it more specific, referring to a particular revelation to a particular family. It is filled with revelations to the family about Africa, mostly revelations which upset their preconceptions. "The Things We Learned," leading up to the proclamation of Congolese independence on June 30, 1960, form the materials of this book.

The third book, entitled "The Judges," is named after the biblical book of Judges, and as with "The Revelation," Kingsolver has added a definite article. This title is more ambiguous than the others, being relevant to judgments made by the members of the Price family on Africa and Africans, as well as to the opposite, to judgments made by Africa and Africans on the family. Both interpretations are possible. The biblical epigraph maintains the ambiguity, for taken from Judges 2:2–3, it bears instructions to avoid making common cause with "the inhabitants of this land" and destroying their altars, but adds that they "shall be as thorns in your sides, and their gods shall be a snare unto you." The subtitle of "The Judges" is "The Things We Didn't Know." Subtitle, epigraph, and main title all emphasize increasing enmity, and all lead inescapably toward the disaster which is to come.

The fourth book is entitled "Bel and the Serpent," the title of an apocryphal passage containing several stories absent in the King James Bible which Nathan uses, but present as an addition to the book of Daniel in Roman Catholic and some Jewish versions. "Bel" is another spelling for the more familiar "Baal," a "heathen" god whose worship was being forced on Daniel and other Jews. Kingsolver's epigraph is from Bel and the Serpent 1:6, which quotes a priest of Bel stating that Bel is a true god for he eats and sleeps, revealing his power to intervene in human affairs. The book's subtitle is "What We Lost," and a sermon from the Apocrypha in which Daniel proves that Bel is a false god is preached by Nathan and leads ironically to the election in which the village votes Christianity out. The village leader cunningly takes his cue from the sermon and calls for an election, bringing together what the Congolese have learned about democratic elections and what they have just heard about ancient competition between religious systems. Ironically, Nathan's values lose, as the villagers declare by their votes that Jesus is not a true god, no more than Bel had been, by implication that Jesus is poisonwood. What the Prices lost, then, was their mission and any hope of prevailing. They also, in a separate but related and parallel action, lose Ruth May as a result of the cleverness of the same village leader.

The meaning of the title of the fifth book, "Exodus," is immediately clear. It refers to the book in which the Hebrews left Egypt and their period of slavery there. The epigraph, from Exodus 13:19–22, concerns their leaving and what they carried away with them. Appropriately, Kingsolver's subtitle is "What We Carried Out." The book, in bringing the stories of the major participants through succeeding years, demonstrates how they were changed by their experiences and what spiritual and emotional scars, values, and lessons have influenced who they have become.

Book six, as noted earlier, differs from all the others in at least one important way, lacking an opening narrative by Orleanna Price. Like book four, however, it is titled from apocryphal material. The apocryphal "Song of the Three Children" is a passage containing a hymn sung by three male youths (Shadrach, Meshach, and Abednego). Kingsolver's epigraph, from Song of the Three Children 7–19, is from the prayer of Azariah (Abednego) in the fiery furnace as he accepts his plight as being part of God's justice and yet expresses faith that God may "deliver us in your wonderful way." Kingsolver adapts the title to refer to her novel's three remaining daughters, each of whom sums up whatever wisdom she now has. They do seem to accept that everything has been for the best, that they have achieved something from their ordeal, although they have also suffered greatly. The elegiac tone of the epigraph is suitable for the materials that Kingsolver presents in this book.

Finally, the last section departs from biblical imagery in its title and lacks any epigraph. In some senses, this is the true "Revelation" for this Poisonwood Bible. The book's title is "The Eyes in the Trees," as indicated earlier, and it not only presents a new perspective (and a new narrative method) but it also mystically reveals a spiritual conclusion to all the events and meanings of the novel. The "eyes in the trees," associated with snakes, had been alluded to as early as Orleanna's opening narrative and are connected with Ruth May, who is killed by a snake. The biblical book of Genesis depicts a serpent as the agent through which the first man and woman are tempted to sin, and although this motif does not become a structural feature in Kingsolver's novel, its relevance is clear. Knowledge of good and evil, brought about as a result of the serpent's tempting, causes the biblical fall, but here it is the final sad result of a tragic, but in certain respects also joyful, experience. This experience finally rises to the level of myth as the "eyes in the trees" watch. When the mother and three daughters try to return to Kilanga, they are told that there is not and never has been any such village. They must give up their attempt to visit Ruth May's final resting place, but at least they do this with forgiveness—of each other and for all the evil which has been visited upon them. Their bible at last becomes one of reconciliation.

A MARXIST READING OF *THE POISONWOOD BIBLE*

Kingsolver once said that *High Tide in Tucson* could have been titled *Barbara the Marxist Takes on Life* and added that she had avoided "the M word" because of the ignorance of Americans, her audience, about the economic inequalities which surround them (Epstein 36). All of her writing is suffused with awareness of these inequalities but, partly because of its setting in postcolonial Africa, *The Poisonwood Bible* is her work most obviously indebted to the insights and theories based on the ideas of Karl Marx and his co-writer Friedrich Engels, nineteenth-century economic and social commentators, and their followers. Marxist criticism, which developed from their thought and applied their ideas to literature, was particularly influential in the United States in the 1930s, the period of the Great Depression. The Depression, with its economic turmoil, made apparent to many writers and critics the great differences between rich and poor, between working and middle classes. For a time, serious literature in this country was full of socially conscious calls for political and economic change which would redistribute wealth from the so-called idle rich to those who, in Marxist theory, were the productive members of society, the workers.

Marxism is a complex set of theories and observations which received their first and most influential expression in two works, *The Communist Manifesto* (1848) by Marx and Engels and *Das Kapital* ("Capital" 1867) by Marx. It can be briefly characterized as a system of thought based on the belief that labor is the primary producer of value. It therefore calls for workers to control the wealth which they produce. Under capitalism, by contrast, it is the employers who control the wealth, and according to Marxist thought, this will lead to inevitable class struggle as the workers try to take what is rightfully theirs. The Marxist argues that not only is this class struggle inevitable, but so too is the eventual victory of the workers, the proletariat, who will finally establish a classless society and the state will wither away. Marxist writers in the United States, since they are living in a capitalist society, depict the evils of that society and call for the class struggle which, they believe, will lead to first a socialist and eventually a communist state in which all property is held in common and there is no injustice. By comparison, Marxist writers in the Soviet Union, describe the victories of their system and attempt to show how history reveals a movement toward the eventual and inevitable communist utopia. Authors writing in or about other nations indicate where their people are on the historical continuum presented by Marxist thought as stretching from the tyranny of the middle class over the workers to the workers' paradise which is ultimately predicted.

Many writers dealing with colonial countries, that is, poor or undeveloped countries controlled by rich and developed nations, combine political and economic arguments. The oppressed people seek to overthrow the alien power that is oppressing them so that they may both establish their own cultural freedom and build just economic and political conditions. It is into this framework that *The Poisonwood Bible* must be set. This novel brings an American family to the Belgian Congo. They are representatives of the powerful West, although not of the specific nation which has had control of the colony and people. They seek to convert the Congolese to their religious beliefs, thus exerting religious control over them, despite their ignorance of the spiritual beliefs and life of those upon whom they would impose their particular brand of conservative Christianity. The ignorance of other aspects of the Congolese people and their lives is equally great, as revealed by the family's inability to make the soil yield the crops they had thought would grow easily if only proper methods were used. They are and remain totally alien to the village in which they live. Throughout the novel the contrast between cultures, with the West assuming its total superiority—an assumption frequently shown to be based on ignorance and wrong—is dramatized.

The time span of the novel, from 1959 to around 1994, is significant. The Price family arrives in Kilanga in 1959, in the final months of colonial rule in the Congo. They learn something of the oppression visited upon ordinary Congolese by a cruel colonial system, and this learning of history continues after independence, as the girls grow up and become more capable of understanding. Independence—and with it chaos—comes on June 30, 1960, but the Price family remains behind despite all calls for evacuation. The obsession of the father controls their lives as completely and insanely as the Belgian exploiters had controlled the rich resources and people of the Congo. Throughout the novel, the confused and often bloody history of the Congo, later called Zaire, is followed, paralleling the experiences of the Price family members, especially those of Leah, the maturest, wisest, and most sympathetic member. Importantly developed through Leah's narration are the great hopes of the early days with the adulation of the first leader, Patrice Lumumba, idolized by revolutionaries, condemned by the Western world as a communist, and killed before his leadership could take real shape. Also depicted is the betrayal of independence under the corrupt Mobutu government. Throughout, the heroic efforts of Anatole, the schoolteacher who becomes Leah's husband, to bring education to his people and his support for freedom and justice remain a constant thread.

Kingsolver's history lesson shows how the hopes of the Congolese people for freedom, peace, and justice were repeatedly thwarted, first by the colonialism of Belgium with its brutal labor system and then by the meddling of the United States in the internal affairs of this new nation. American fears of communism throughout the period of the Cold War motivated this interference. These points are the most obvious expression of Marxist attitudes in *The Poisonwood Bible*. But in other ways, those notions pervade the novel. A few brief examples may suffice. The characterization of Rachel as a useless and shallow but decorative woman is an illustration of one way in which middle-class women are often portrayed by Marxists. Her concern only for herself and her ability to see everything only as it affects her are typical, as is her exploiting her own beauty, using it to live off a succession of men. Even when she becomes independent and builds a life for herself in an economically productive way, by running a hotel, she makes the hotel an instrument of discrimination, catering only to the white, wealthy, and powerful, even though that means her own brother-in-law cannot be a visitor. She has no scruples about refusing Anatole service, although she does provide some minimal services for blacks behind the hotel. She learns nothing, defending the United States and its interference in Africa until the end of the novel.

Other characters significantly represent other phenomena relevant to a Marxist reading of the novel. Eeben Axelroot, totally corrupt, willing to buy, smuggle, or sell anything, and eager to participate in any activity that may make him money, is an extreme example of what colonial exploiters can become. Anatole and Leah, with their love of the Congolese people, function as opposites to Rachel and Eeben. Throughout, there is the contrast between Western plenty and Congolese poverty, with the points being made repeatedly that the West has no understanding of the Congo and that its presence there can only corrupt and spoil what the Congolese people might build if they were only given the chance.

The inevitability of a victory by the Africans, in keeping with the Marxist belief in the final victory of the proletariat, seems foretold by the novel in several ways. Africa is a force which overcomes all the best efforts of the obsessive and finally insane Nathan Price; it has destroyed him. But it also has become home to two of his daughters, one who has lovingly embraced its land and people, and one who is forever foreign but cannot return to her native land because she is equally foreign there. The third daughter has made a life for herself in the United States, but even her life is directed by her African experience as she specializes in tropical medicine. At the end of the novel a disembodied voice speaks. That voice comes from the "eyes in the trees" (which Orleanna had asked the reader to become in her opening passage), from Ruth May, the fourth daughter, who is buried in African soil and is now one with it, and from Africa itself, the final power here. The final line, in what might be seen as a Marxist and also mystical optimism about final triumph, foresees freedom from the sins and pains of the past and reads, "Move on. Walk forward into the light" (543).

Bibliography

WORKS BY BARBARA KINGSOLVER

Animal Dreams. 1990. New York: HarperPerennial, 1991.

Another America/Otra America. With Spanish translations by Rebeca Cartes. Seattle: Seal Press, 1992.

The Bean Trees. 1988. New York: HarperPerennial, 1992.

High Tide in Tucson: Essays from Now or Never. New York: HarperCollins, 1995.

Holding the Line: Women in the Great Arizona Mine Strike of 1983. 1989. New York: ILR Press, 1996.

Homeland and Other Stories. 1989. New York: HarperPerennial, 1993.

"My Father's Africa." *McCall's* August 1991: 115–23.

Pigs in Heaven. 1993. New York: HarperPerennial, 1994.

The Poisonwood Bible. New York: HarperFlamingo, 1998.

"The Prince Thing." *Woman's Day* 18 February 1992: 26, 28, 110.

"Rose-Johnny: A Story." *The Virginia Quarterly Review* 63.1 (winter 1987): 88–109.

"Untitled." In *Letters to Our Mothers: I've Always Meant to Tell You: An Anthology of Contemporary Women Writers*. Ed. Constance Warloe. New York: Pocket Books, 1997.

"The Way We Are." In "A Parenting Special Report." *Parenting* March 1995: 74–81.

"Women on the Line." With Jill Barrett Fein. *The Progressive* March 1984: 15.

WORKS ABOUT BARBARA KINGSOLVER

General Information

"Barbara Kingsolver." *Signature* series of interviews on PBS. Produced at the University of Kentucky, 1997.

Epstein, Robin. "*The Progressive* Interview: Barbara Kingsolver." *The Progressive* February 1996: 33–37.

Farrell, Michael J. "In Life, Art, Writer Plumbs Politics of Hope." *National Catholic Reporter* 22 May 1992: 21, 29–30.

Fleischner, Jennifer. *A Reader's Guide to the Fiction of Barbara Kingsolver.* New York: HarperPerennial, 1994.

Hile, Janet L. "Barbara Kingsolver." *Authors & Artists.* Vol. 15: 73–79.

Perry, Donna. *Backtalk: Women Writers Speak Out: Interviews.* New Brunswick: Rutgers University Press, 1993. 143–69.

Quinn, Judy. "Book News: HarperCollins Gets to Keep Kingsolver." *Publishers Weekly* 10 February 1997: 19. See also Kingsolver's response: "Kingsolver Clarifies." *Publishers Weekly* 7 April 1997: 11.

Ross, Jean W. "Kingsolver, Barbara." *Contemporary Authors.* Vol. 134: 284–90.

Ryan, Maureen. "Barbara Kingsolver's Lowfat Fiction." *Journal of American Culture* 18.4 (winter 1995): 77–82.

See, Lisa. "PW Interviews Barbara Kingsolver." *Publishers Weekly* 31 August 1990: 46–47.

REVIEWS AND CRITICISM OF NOVELS

The Bean Trees

"Briefly Noted: Fiction: The Bean Trees." *The New Yorker* 4 April 1988: 101–2.

Butler, Jack. "She Hung the Moon and Plugged in All the Stars." *The New York Times Book Review* 10 April 1988: 15.

Fitzgerald, Karen. "A Major New Talent." *Ms.* April 1988: 28.

Manuel, Diane. "A Roundup of First Novels about Coming of Age." *Christian Science Monitor* 22 April 1988: 20.

Mossman, Robert. "The Bean Trees." *Library Journal* December 1994: 85.

Randall, Margaret. "Human Comedy." *Women's Review of Books* May 1988: 1, 3.

Animal Dreams

Aay, Henry. "Environmental Themes in Ecofiction: *In the Center of the Nation* and *Animal Dreams.*" *Journal of Cultural Geography* 14.2 (spring/summer 1994): 65–85.

"Animal Dreams." *Publishers Weekly* 22 June 1990: 45.

Keymer, David. "Kingsolver, Barbara. Animal Dreams." *Library Journal* August 1990: 143.

Newman, Vicky. "Compelling Ties: Landscape, Community, and Sense of Place." *Peabody Journal of Education* 70.4 (summer 1995): 105–18.

Smiley, Jane. "In One Small Town, the Weight of the World." *The New York Times Book Review* 2 September 1990: 2.

Pigs in Heaven

Karbo, Karen. "And Baby Makes Two." *The New York Times Book Review* 27 June 1993: 9.

Lamb, Lynette. "Pigs in Heaven." *Utne Reader* July/August 1993: 122.

McCormack-Lee, Marlene. "Kingsolver, Barbara. Pigs in Heaven." *Library Journal* 15 June 1993: 97.

"*Pigs in Heaven.*" *Publishers Weekly* 5 April 1993: 62.

Scott, Mary. "Solomon's Wisdom." *New Statesman & Society* 10 December 1993: 40.

Sheppard, R. Z. "Little Big Girl." *Time* 30 August 1993: 65.

The Poisonwood Bible

"Forecasts: *The Poisonwood Bible.*" *Publishers Weekly* 10 August 1998: 366.

Kakutani, Michiko. "No Ice Cream Cones in a Heart of Darkness." *New York Times* 16 October 1998: B43.

Kerr, Sarah. "The Novel as Indictment." *The New York Times Magazine* 11 October 1998: 53–55.

Klinkerborg, Verlyn. "Going Native." *The New York Times Book Review* 18 October 1998: 7.

Quinn, Judy. "Book News: HarperCollins Gets to Keep Kingsolver." *Publishers Weekly* 10 February 1997: 19. See also Kingsolver's response: "Kingsolver Clarifies." *Publishers Weekly* 7 April 1997: 11.

REVIEWS AND CRITICISM OF OTHER WORKS

Holding the Line: Women in the Great Arizona Mine Strike of 1983

Rozen, Frieda Shoenberg. "Social Science: Kingsolver, Barbara. Holding the Line: Women in the Great Arizona Mine Strike in [sic] 1983." *Library Journal* 1 November 1989: 104.

Stegner, Page. "Both Sides Lost." *The New York Times Book Review* 7 January 1990: 31.

Tischler, Barbara L. *"Holding the Line: Women in the Great Arizona Mine Strike of 1983."* *Labor Studies Journal* spring 1992: 82–83.

Homeland and Other Stories

Banks, Russell. "Distant as a Cherokee Childhood." *The New York Times Book Review* 11 June 1989: 16.

Zindel, Timothy L. "Kingsolver, Barbara. Homeland and Other Stories." *Library Journal* 15 May 1989: 90.

Another America/Otra America

McKee, Louis. "Another America: Otra America." *Library Journal* 1 April 1998: 92.

Ratner, Rochelle. "Poetry: Kingsolver, Barbara." *Library Journal* 15 February 1992: 171.

Roses, Lorraine Elena. "Language and Other Barriers: *Another America/Otra America."* *Women's Review of Books* July 1992: 42.

High Tide in Tucson

King, Casey. "Books in Brief: Nonfiction." *The New York Times Book Review* 15 October 1995.

Seaman, Donna. "Upfront: Advance Reviews: Kingsolver, Barbara." *Booklist* 1 September 1995: 2–3.

Stevens, Penny. "Kingsolver, Barbara. *High Tide in Tucson."* *School Library Journal* February 1996: 134.

Trachtman, Paul. "Book Reviews: *High Tide in Tucson."* *Smithsonian* June 1996: 24.

Index

About the Author

MARY JEAN DeMARR is Professor Emerita of English and Women's Studies at Indiana State University. She is the author of *Colleen McCullough* (Greenwood, 1996) and the co-author of *Adolescent Female Portraits in the American Novel 1961–1981* (1983) and *The Adolescent in the American Novel Since 1960* (1986).